"My immediate response when I read the manuscript was, 'This book is a must!' It put many of my personal thoughts, beliefs, and convictions into words and practical applications. It is simple enough to understand. Jesus said, 'If ye love me, keep my commandments.' Our Old Order churches rightly stress that importance. Yet, the commandment of the last commission has mostly been limited to the teaching of letting our light shine by visible separation. This book should help broaden our views without compromising our faith. Churches that fail to follow the command to evangelize are often plagued with inward strife that darkens the light to the lost and dying world. Being the 'quiet of the land' is not a virtue of advance when it comes to spreading the Gospel of Jesus Christ, but rather a 'bushel' of retreat that hides the light intended to light the world. May God use this book to rekindle that light."

–*Michigan Bishop*

"A refreshing and inspiring read. Why so? The author articulates very well a deficiency among us. I appreciate how he offers solutions to the need, yet always within the Old Order setting...May the Lord be merciful to us! May we allow Him to help us repair the 'wheel' that is weakened."

–*Michigan Bishop*

"I can endorse the writing as scriptural and practical...I have often wondered why 'evangelism' had such a negative outcome. Joshua Zimmerman's conclusions have satisfied me...We are reactionists by nature; it's so much easier. The 'evangelism' subject is an example in case. This book...has caused me to take a fresh, honest look at the subject...Some of our internal strife may be the result of our inward focus of exclusiveness, and yet we must not embrace ecumenism. The scriptures have the answer."

–Ohio Minister

"I consider this an excellent writing on a sensitive subject. I would highly recommend it to be read by all members of the 'plain' churches. It has a clear call to examine our focus and purpose in the light of God's Word instead of on... opinion or preference. It is challenging, not condemning. By comparing evangelizing to a spoke in a wheel, the author invites us to look at our entire 'wheel'. He takes us on a thoughtful journey undergirded by Christ's teachings and made vibrant with lessons, examples, triumphs, and failures from history. Let everyone take the message to heart (instead of shooting the messenger) and strengthen the weak areas in their setting. Let the Kingdom advance...as long as time remains. Let us be building bridges with appropriate guard rails and not walls."

–Michigan Minister

The
Missing
SP🞧KE

A Fresh, Honest Look at Christ's Last Commission

Joshua Zimmerman

THE MISSING SPOKE: A Fresh, Honest Look at Christ's
Last Commission

Published in cooperation with Old Order Amish Literature
Fund (OOALF)

*Additional copies can
be requested from:*
Ridgeway Books for OOALF
3161 Fruit Avenue
Medina, NY 14103

ISBN:978-0-9988824-0-6

Printed in the United States of America

Printing service by:
Pilgrim Book Printing
Medina, New York
(888) 822-7894

Table of Contents

PREFACE

The year was A.D. 30 in a small town in the Middle East. Little did the Jews in that town realize to what extent their lives would soon be changed. A wilderness man, clothed in a camel skin and leather belt, began preaching, "Repent ye: for the kingdom of heaven is at hand" (Matthew 3:2).

Shortly afterward, a relative of John the Baptist appeared, preaching the same message. He said, "Repent: for the kingdom of heaven is at hand" (Matthew 4:17).

For the next three years, the people in Galilee and nearby regions found their religious beliefs shaken. Not everybody accepted the radical message. This Prophet and King stepped on toes and crossed cultural lines. Finally some people could stand it no longer, and they condemned Him to die as a criminal.

Jesus' teachings were indeed radical. His message was unlike any other, and His kingdom unlike any earthly kingdom.

Jesus expected a drastic change in the lives of His disciples. After an eventful three years of ministry, Jesus commissioned them, saying, "Go ye therefore, and teach all nations, baptizing them in the name of the Father, and of the Son, and of the Holy Ghost: teaching them to observe all things whatsoever I have commanded you" (Matthew 28:19–20).

Some give this passage, along with Mark 16:15–16, a prominent place, and refer to it as the Great Commission. Since this term is not in the Bible, we will simply refer to these parting words as "Christ's last commission."[1]

While there are exceptions, Old Order[2] groups have felt that this commission was largely a mandate for the original apostles. We have not completely refrained from reaching out to those outside our circles, but the theory that this commission is apostolic has affected our duty to unbelievers.[3]

What you are about to read may seem radical. Yet it surely is not as radical as Jesus' teachings seemed to the Jews. I do not promote dropping *Gelassenheit* in favor of Pietism.[4] But how can we regain the vision of evangelistic outreach without sacrificing other precious values? That is the essence of this book.

I do not consider myself a professional historian. Much of the history in this book is from the work of others. If my summary is not accurate, my sources may have been faulty. I believe we must be willing to study history and learn from it

---

[1] Except when quoting from other writers' works.
[2] The Old Order movement began in the late nineteenth and early twentieth centuries, when traditionally-inclined leaders objected to the changes and innovations coming into the plain churches. The Old Order movement began in the 1860s–1870s among the Amish. Among the Mennonites, it began in Indiana in 1872; in Ontario, 1889; in Pennsylvania, 1893; and in Virginia, 1901. Sunday schools, English preaching, prolonged revival meetings, and missions were the prominent innovations. Considering this phase of history helps us understand why the relationship between the Old Order and outreach remains delicate and controversial.
[3] We must give credit where credit is due. Various Old Order individuals are reaching out in commendable ways.
[4] The German word *Gelassenheit* has no English equivalent. Roughly translated, it means "submission and surrender, first to God, but also to our brethren." Pietism, on the other hand, minimizes church authority in favor of personal religious experience.

in light of the Bible. As we study, we must keep in mind that God's Word is the ultimate authority, no matter what story the past has written.

Last but not least, I recognize I cannot altogether avoid stepping on some toes or crossing cherished boundaries. I desire to remain friends even if we must disagree. I realize that those who cling to the traditional "Old Order" perspective of mission work also possess insights that must not be overlooked. Let us not allow animosity to develop; we need each other. We want to be part of that "great multitude . . . of all nations, and kindreds, and people, and tongues" standing before God's throne, clothed in white robes and holding palms in our hands.[5]

—Joshua Zimmerman

---

[5] Revelation 7:9.

FOREWORD

More than three thousand years ago, a wise man penned words that aptly sum up the message of this book. "Where there is no vision, the people perish: but he that keepeth the law, happy is he" (Proverbs 29:18). A careful study of the original language suggests the following meaning: Where there is no perception of the will of God, the people become as nothing through lack of commitment and restraint; but those who keep the commandments will be blessed.

Twice a year at communion, we hear these words: *"Der Sinn, Bild, und Natur Christus teilhaftig zu sein"* (Be partakers of Christ's mind, image, and character). If we desire the mind of Christ, we will drop our passiveness concerning the "missing spoke" in obedience to Christ's commands; we will become active concerning the lost around us. Jesus did not wait until people came to Him; He went to them. He said of Himself, "For the Son of man is come to seek and to save that which was lost" (Luke 19:10).

As I reflected on the author's excellent analogy of the wheel, with Jesus as the hub, my mind went further. Without the hub, there can be no wheel. Yet a wheel can be used with a spoke missing, at least for some time. Extended use with a spoke out weakens the other spokes, and eventually the wheel becomes unusable. And what about the outer band of the wheel? Is it not the love of God, binding everything together? "And above all these things put on charity, which is the bond of perfectness" (Colossians 3:14). The Luther German refers to *"das Band der Vollkommenheit,"* or the band of perfectness.

My children recently witnessed firsthand the importance of the outer band on a carriage wheel. While traveling home, one of the bands fell completely off. They thought it comical to head on home while riding on the spokes alone. However, they could not have gone much farther before ruining all the spokes.

Consider with me the "spokes" of a functioning church. First, we have the seven ordinances. When I counted other key facets of the Scriptural/Anabaptist church, I realized my list numbered sixteen—the number of spokes in our carriage wheels!

A full-length book could be written on each of these facets:

1. Communion
2. Baptism
3. Anointing with oil
4. Holy kiss
5. Marriage
6. Feet-washing
7. Christian woman's veiling
8. Nonresistance
9. *Gelassenheit*
10. Work ethic
11. Family unit

12. Nonconformity
13. Priesthood of all believers
14. New birth
15. Cross-bearing
16. Evangelistic outreach

None of these are complete in themselves, but properly put together they become a beautiful unit representing Christ to fallen man. Eternity will reflect the results as we take our duty regarding all sixteen "spokes" seriously.

Are we compelled to open our hearts and, with the mind of Christ, to reach out? It will require vision. Our introversive minds could use a change. As in all angles of the Christian walk, caution must be exercised. With proper oversight, our mature youth could experience spiritual growth if they would be included in outreach.

For myself, I am grateful that about ten generations ago, the Mennonite Church in Switzerland received my Martin ancestor. Since then, the doors of various plain churches have become more restricted. I would like to see them opened enough again to encourage true seekers to enter. I want to do my part. To echo the idea of Saint Francis of Assisi, "Preach the Gospel always; use words when necessary." May we be found faithful.

—*Kenton Martin*

Chapter One

Whose Kingdom?

Is Success Proof of God's Blessing?

The year was 1489. The Waldenses, living in the valleys of the Piedmont of southern France, were rejoicing. They were finally allowed by the duke of Savoy to live in peace. Only two years earlier, the Waldenses were executed by the thousands for refusing to join the state church. Determined to wipe out this heretical sect, the duke of Savoy had gathered 18,000 soldiers and killed several thousand Waldenses, including women and children. How successful the duke and his soldiers would have been in terminating the Waldensian movement remains unknown. One historian noted that in a certain area, nearly everyone fled except for a core group who decided to stay and fight the soldiers.[6] Le Noir of Mondovi, also referred to as "Nero of Mondovi," was an officer of the army. He and his soldiers

---

[6] "The Waldensians," http://www.thereformation.info/waldensians.htm.

attacked these Waldensian farmers, who only had bows and arrows and homemade wooden and leather shields. When the Waldenses realized what was happening, they fell to their knees and raised their arms, crying, "O God of our fathers, help us!"[7] As Nero of Mondovi raised his visor to yell a taunt at them, a Waldensian youth aimed an arrow at his forehead. The officer fell. With renewed vigor, the Waldensian farmers attacked the soldiers, killing many.

Sometime later, the remaining soldiers regrouped. Approaching the mountain where the Waldenses were hiding, the soldiers prepared to attack. Suddenly a cloud formation on the summit of the mountain expanded and descended into the gorge, darkening it. Recognizing their advantage, the Waldenses emerged from their hiding places and scattered all over the mountain. They threw rocks into the gorge onto the army. Others entered the gorge, assaulting the soldiers. The troops panicked. Some trampled on their fellow soldiers, while others drowned in the river.

During the next year, the Waldenses continued their attacks until they managed to wipe out most of the soldiers. Finally the duke of Savoy declared peace.

Those of us who are familiar with early Waldensian history can't help wondering what happened to their nonresistance. Three hundred years earlier, the Waldenses, also known as the "poor men of Lyons," had faced persecution as they endeavored to obey Jesus' command to "Love your enemies, bless them that curse you, do good to them that hate you, and pray for them which despitefully

---

[7] J.A. Wiley, *The History of the Waldenses*, 12.

use you, and persecute you" (Matthew 5:44).

We wonder, did any of these Waldenses question whether fighting against the soldiers was the right thing to do? Perhaps no one remembered when their people had begun to compromise concerning Jesus' example of nonresistance. By this time, the Waldenses were compromising in other ways too. Since they were not allowed to buy or sell in the public markets, many of them were partaking of mass and allowing their children to be baptized in the Catholic Church.

Some historians conclude that God blessed the Waldenses' military efforts. They liken the incident of the youth shooting Nero of Mondovi to the Bible story of David and Goliath. The incident of the cloud formation is seen as proof that God was on the Waldenses' side.

Other historians see it differently. One historian remarked, "The Waldensians [were] allowed . . . to continue unmolested in their valley homes; but only for a short while as the priests and Inquisitors rallied for their more pernicious attacks."[8]

Of course, we believe that the Waldenses had abandoned one of the pillars of their faith. Just as a wheel with a missing spoke is weakened, so their faith was weakened by abandoning a Scriptural principle.

Could we say that other groups throughout history— including our plain churches—have gradually lost one or more "spokes of their wheels"?

---

[8] "The Waldensians," http://www.thereformation.info/waldensians.htm.

Is Our Lifestyle and Our Evangelistic Witness One and the Same?

Should we be developing a vision for reaching out? Or is our example and lifestyle an adequate witness? The Bible teaches that Christians should be examples whose lives are consistent with what they profess. Although our lifestyle, apparel, and practices can be a witness, many outsiders[9] can detect whether or not our faith is authentic.

We have always valued a consistent lifestyle and example. But is it possible that we have minimized other equally significant Scripture passages that command us to reach out and help others enter the kingdom of God?

We of Anabaptist heritage confess that the Gospel is for all men, regardless of race, background, language, or culture. "The Lord is not slack concerning his promise, as some men count slackness; but is longsuffering to us-ward, not willing that any should perish, but that all should come to repentance" (2 Peter 3:9). Is this our vision? Or do we tend to think that we are God's favored people today, as the Jews were in the Old Testament? As precious as our heritage should be, we cannot claim salvation through our heritage, and we must not keep others from salvation because of it.

It seems that the reasons for not evangelizing are diverse. If we asked ten different people why some plain churches do not actively evangelize, we might receive ten different answers. Here are some possible reasons:

1. Christ's last commission was fulfilled by the apostles.

2. We believe that our most effective witness is in how

---

[9] In this treatise, the term *outsiders* refers to those who are outside the boundaries of conservative Anabaptist circles, whether or not they are believers.

we live, raise our families, and earn a living through hard work.

3. It is not that we don't evangelize at all; the apostle Peter wrote that we must be ready to give an answer to someone who asks about our faith.

4. The reason we don't actively evangelize is because we are nonresistant.

5. Outreach is not in harmony with our emphasis on humility.

6. It would never work to proselytize outsiders to our way of life; our culture and theirs are too different.

7. Our churches would never be able to adapt to foreign cultures.

8. Outreach is a threat to our values and lifestyle.

9. The liberal Mennonites emphasized outreach, and look where they are now!

10. The Scriptures nowhere command us to engage in outreach in order to be saved.

Some individuals in plain circles see nothing wrong with outreach in any form. They respect and appreciate what some organizations and churches are doing. They contribute funds to Christian Aid Ministries and other reputable charitable organizations. Yet they see no value in becoming more active. For too long, evangelistic work has been viewed as foreign to traditional theology, and too many of us are satisfied to leave it that way.

It is not in the scope of this writing to judge or condemn various Old Order groups for this standpoint. Various factors in history have molded this branch of the Christian church for what it is today. (I will discuss this further in Chapter 11.) Rather, the question I wish to explore is this: How can we regain the vision for evangelistic outreach within the scope of a traditional lifestyle and structure?

God's Chosen People: The Kingdom

God chose the Israelites to be a separate and peculiar people from the nations around them. Prior to their entry into Canaan, Moses said, "For thou art an holy people unto the LORD thy God: the LORD thy God hath chosen thee to be a special people unto himself, above all people that are upon the face of the earth" (Deuteronomy 7:6).

This was the kingdom of Israel: a literal kingdom with political laws and officials who, at God's command, used executive authority to subdue the Gentile nations and to keep order within their own ranks. But time and again they forgot God and learned the ways of their heathen neighbors. Because of their disobedience, God eventually allowed the Babylonian and Assyrian armies to carry them into captivity. Only a remnant ever returned to their native land.

Like the Israelites, Christians today are God's people. Israel's separation from the ungodly nations around them was a type of the separation required of the Christian church today. However, the church is not a political kingdom like the Israelites. It is a higher kingdom—a spiritual kingdom. Both John the Baptist and Jesus preached, "Repent: for the kingdom of heaven is at hand."[10]

To define His kingdom, Jesus laid out some requirements. Only the poor in spirit, the mournful, the

---

[10] Matthew 3:2; 4:17.

meek, the spiritually hungry and thirsty, the merciful, the pure in heart, the peacemakers, and the persecuted qualify to enter this kingdom. The citizens of this kingdom are the salt of the earth and the light of the world.

Jesus explained the differences between the Mosaic Law and His kingdom. For example, men would be judged not only for committing the literal act of murder, but also for harboring unresolved anger against a brother. Not only was the outward act of adultery sin, but so were lustful thoughts. Remarriage was not permitted as long as the former spouse was living. Swearing was not allowed. The citizens of Christ's kingdom were to be truthful at all times. Retaliation was not a part of Christ's kingdom.

In Matthew 5:45, Jesus taught why these precepts were necessary: "That ye may be the children of your Father which is in heaven."

Jesus also admonished His disciples, "If any man desire to be first, the same shall be last of all, and servant of all" (Mark 9:35). To illustrate this concept, Jesus called a young child into their midst and told them that only those who humble themselves and become like little children can enter His kingdom. (See also Matthew 18:3–4.)

What is Jesus' kingdom like? He said, "The kingdom of heaven is like to a grain of mustard seed, which a man took, and sowed in his field: which indeed is the least of all seeds: but when it is grown, it is the greatest among herbs, and becometh a tree, so that the birds of the air come and lodge in the branches thereof" (Matthew 13:31–32). Christ's kingdom started with a despised beginning but has mushroomed into something immeasurably great.

Are We Blind?

Jesus proclaimed the essence of His kingdom when He spoke to Pilate: "My kingdom is not of this world: if my kingdom were of this world, then would my servants fight, that I should not be delivered to the Jews: but now is my kingdom not from hence" (John 18:36). This raises a question: How could the Jews have been so blind as to misunderstand the essence of His kingdom? They anticipated a literal kingdom similar to their former kingdom of Israel. They assumed Jesus would be a powerful ruler, overcoming the Roman kingdom by force. How mistaken they were!

Likewise, the Waldenses were blind because they ignored one of the foundational pillars of Jesus' kingdom. By defending themselves, they were not representing Christ's kingdom at all. They were defending their own kingdom.

Today many professing Christians are also blind because they do not grasp the essence of Christ's kingdom. Some denominations believe that in Christ's literal premillenial reign on earth, His teachings will be obligatory; but at this time, His teachings are merely ideal.

This brings us to a startling question: Are we also blind? Do we grasp the essence of Christ's kingdom? Or are we building a kingdom—an "Amish or Mennonite"—that, while separated from the world's kingdoms by conformity to the basic teachings of Jesus, is marked by our own biased preferences?

Jesus did not come to give another law like the Law of Moses, nor another temporal kingdom like the kingdom of Israel. We should become aware of the pitfall of building an Amish or Mennonite kingdom that we think will bring us salvation. When we grasp the spirit of Jesus' teachings, we adopt His mindset. This means giving ourselves for the good of others. We are adept at making this concept work within our own families and the brotherhood. But should it stop there?

This is the big question for our plain churches. Is it enough to obey Christ's teachings within a counterculture such as we have? Or do we also have a responsibility to outsiders who do not know what the kingdom of God means? If they were taught the basic concept of Christ's kingdom, they would more easily grasp Jesus' commands such as nonresistance and separation from the world.

Jesus' purpose for coming to earth—to establish His kingdom—was not restricted to setting a good example. It included showing men the way to salvation. Jesus clarified His mission to Zacchaeus, saying, "For the Son of man is come to seek and to save that which was lost" (Luke 19:10). Is this not also part of the church's mission today—to seek the lost?

Our example and lifestyle do play a part in extending Christ's kingdom. Eternity will reveal the souls who have entered the kingdom as a result of that. However, our vision for the church must be Scriptural, or we will be unable to call others to receive the essence of Christ's kingdom.

So what does His kingdom include, besides being separate from the world and obeying Christ's teachings within our own subculture? Consider Luke 4:18–19: "The Spirit of the Lord is upon me, because he hath anointed me to preach the gospel to the poor; he hath sent me to heal the brokenhearted, to preach deliverance to the captives, and recovering of sight to the blind, to set at liberty them that are bruised, to preach the acceptable year of the Lord."

This passage describes in a nutshell Christ's mission on earth. The Christian church is the arm of Christ to preach the Gospel, to call sinners to repentance, and to exhort believers. Her duty extends further than her immediate membership and posterity.

The Mind of Christ

Mortals cannot grasp the complete, infinite mind of God and how He relates to mankind. We can only comprehend a small part of His love, mercy, and care for the human race. The apostle Paul acknowledged, "O the depth of the riches both of the wisdom and knowledge of God! how unsearchable are his judgments, and his ways past finding out! For who hath known the mind of the Lord? or who hath been his counsellor?" (Romans 11:33–34). So great is God's love for mankind that He ". . . is longsuffering to us-ward, not willing that any should perish, but that all should come to repentance" (2 Peter 3:9).

God is no respecter of persons. He does not favor a certain race, nationality, or tribe. Peter, in his encounter with Cornelius, acknowledged, "Of a truth I perceive that God is no respecter of persons: but in every nation he that feareth him, and worketh righteousness, is accepted with him" (Acts 10:34–35). God loves every soul alike; He shows no partiality. Neither should we. This is one reason various plain churches should be doing more evangelistic outreach. Jesus Christ has the same mind as God the Father, and He is the Head of the church. As a result, His followers should also adopt this same compassion.

Let's look at Philippians 2:5–8: "Let this mind be in you, which was also in Christ Jesus: who, being in the form of God, thought it not robbery to be equal with God: but made himself of no reputation, and took upon him the form of a servant, and was made in the likeness of men: and being found in fashion as a man, he humbled himself, and became obedient unto death, even the death of the cross." Here we see the mind of Christ. Although He was a king, He willingly humbled Himself to a servant's position. Having the mind of the Father, He could not bear to see mankind lost. Therefore, He came to earth to reconcile them to God. This is the nature of the kingdom of Jesus Christ.

Jesus left a shining example for the citizens of His kingdom. He had compassion on humanity and went out of His way to reconcile them to God. He did it because He knew that they were condemned to eternal death. Do we, the citizens of His kingdom, have the same vision?

What If . . . ?

What world would we live in today if Jesus had thought of His mission in this manner? "My Father sent me to this earth to reconcile men to Him. But it will never work for me to go and preach to the people. I would constantly be stirring up resentment and strife. That won't work; my Father sent me to be a peacemaker. While some people might agree with me, many won't. The last thing I want to do is to cause a split among my people. The elders will never accept such nonsense. They will convince everyone that the old covenant is good enough. It will never work to bring the Jews, Samaritans, and Gentiles into one faith. Too many differences exist in their cultures. Too many of my people might become confused and allow the heathen practices of the Gentiles to influence them. This has happened so often in the past.

"So here is my conclusion. I intend to be a good example to everyone in Nazareth as I quietly go about my work in the carpenter shop and wherever else I happen to be. Everyone will observe my integrity and will want to follow my example as they observe my life and actions from day to day. After all, they say a person's example speaks so loudly, you can't hear what he's saying. I will love my enemies and do good to those who hate me. Whenever someone strikes me on one cheek, I will offer him the other. If someone asks for my cloak, I will offer him my coat also. If someone steals my possessions, even if I know who the thief is, I will not demand that he give them back. If someone knocks out my eye or my tooth, I will not knock out his. I will treat such people kindly because I love them.

"If I went out and preached, people might misunderstand what I meant to tell them. Or I might be tempted to attract honor to myself. But they will never misunderstand my good example. By living a blameless and consistent life, everyone should be able to figure out who I am."

Certainly, Jesus' preaching of the kingdom would hardly have been effective if His walk of life had not measured up consistently. Yet if Jesus had followed the reasoning above, He likely would have escaped death by crucifixion. How then would the way of salvation have been brought to mankind?

Christ's Example of Outreach

Jesus' life, mission, and calling were unusual. He established the New Covenant, rendering the Old Covenant obsolete. The New Covenant proceeded in ways that often seemed the opposite of what people expected.

Remarkably, Jesus' ministry spanned only the last tenth of His earthly life. Were His thirty previous years wasted? Certainly not. This example reminds us that outstanding results are more likely to occur when we wait for God's timing, rather than moving ahead on our own.

Jesus did not boast of His deeds. He never coerced anyone into believing that He was the Christ. He did not fulfill His mission in a highhanded way. He did not employ messengers on chariots or ships to broadcast His message to the people. He did not start any seminary to train missionaries to continue His ministry. Neither did He write books on how to most effectively reach the lost. Jesus focused on training a small group of disciples. When He appeared in the powerful courts of the Roman Empire, it was as a "criminal" with a death sentence.

In the last three years of His life, Jesus' ministry was a life of unselfish sacrifice. He did not allow His quiet example to be His only witness. Had He remained in Nazareth during those years, the sacrifice would not have been as great.

What Christ Required During His Earthly Mission

Christ's life on earth and the lives of His disciples were obviously different from our lives. The Scriptures indicate that not all citizens of Christ's kingdom are required to literally forsake their occupations, homes, and families for the sake of Christ's kingdom. If God has not clearly led us to abandon it all, we are hardly in error to consider our daily work as part of building Christ's kingdom. Opportunities to witness come up at home.

Nevertheless, let us explore some radical requirements Jesus expected of His disciples—requirements that caused His disciples to make drastic sacrifices.

One requirement Jesus laid out for His disciples was that they must become "fishers of men." Simon Peter and Andrew, as well as James and John, made their living by fishing. Fishing was an honest livelihood, but when Jesus called them to be His disciples, they forsook their nets and boats and immediately followed Him.

How willing are we to give up our daily work, farm, or business to work in Christ's kingdom?

A rich young ruler asked Jesus what he must do to inherit eternal life. This man had faithfully kept the Ten Commandments ever since his youth. In our way of thinking, his faithful example should have been sufficient. According to Jesus' theology, all was not well in this man's life. His upright example was not sufficient. This account shows that Jesus expects more of His followers than simply doing good deeds. Our understanding regarding material wealth is in wide contrast to how Jesus taught and practiced it. For this rich ruler, selling out for Christ meant a tremendous sacrifice. In our usual way of thinking, he wouldn't have needed to make that sacrifice if he had simply obeyed Jesus' other basic teachings.

Do we feel too snug within the boundaries of our lifestyle and traditions? God could easily, through adverse circumstances, force us to leave our homes, possessions, occupations, families, and all that we have been used to. A day might be coming in which, because of our faith, we may be forced to flee with nothing but the clothes on our backs. Testings of this kind will then either make or break our faith in God.

I hope we are willing to deny ourselves some comforts occasionally in order to reach out to others. Jesus left the glories of heaven to reach out to us. We as the church are Christ's body. Are we willing to point the masses of lost souls to salvation, as Christ was willing to do?

In summary, when Jesus called His followers, He called them to a life of active service. He did not merely require that they passively consent to be an example to others by adhering to His basic teachings. In other words, Jesus did not recline in the background and relay to His people that if they wanted to find out more about His mission, they could look Him up and He would then gladly teach them whatever they were open to hearing.

Jesus Christ desires that those who represent Him take initiative in reaching lost souls, just as He did. This must be the vision of the New Testament church. If we simply convey that if people want to know more about the true church, they can ask us, are we really following Christ's example? Could our lack of evangelistic outreach stem from self-centeredness?

Chapter Two

Were the Early Christians
Evangelistic?

In the first chapter, we explored how God's kingdom changed from a political kingdom to a spiritual kingdom—a kingdom "not of this world." During the Old Testament era, God's people were usually shown as passive witnesses. The occasional exception happened when God anointed a prophet or gave an audible injunction to someone to speak His message.

But Christ set an example of witnessing actively: He spread His doctrines throughout the cities and villages of Judea, Samaria, and Galilee, which in time would have an impact on the Gentiles. The spiritual kingdom of Christ was not intended to be an exclusively passive witness. Before He ascended to heaven, He commissioned His disciples: "Go ye therefore, and teach all nations, baptizing them in the name of the Father, and of the Son, and of the Holy Ghost: teaching them to observe all things whatsoever I have commanded you: and, lo, I am with you alway, even unto the end of the world" (Matthew 28:19–20).

This was the method of the kingdom of Christ, and it continues today, "even unto the end of the world." No longer are God's people commissioned to make war against the nations of the earth. They are now commissioned to make spiritual war against all earthly kingdoms—to evangelize all earthly nations and kingdoms.

Although most histories of missions cover the Great Awakening, this does not mean that Christians before this avoided evangelizing. The book of Acts records much evangelistic activity of the early Christians. When Saul initiated a mass persecution against the Christians in Jerusalem, many of them dispersed. "Therefore they that were scattered abroad went every where preaching the word" (Acts 8:4). Eventually some Gentiles at Antioch became believers because of their message.

The apostle Paul wrote to the Thessalonians, "For from you sounded out the word of the Lord not only in Macedonia and Achaia, but also in every place your faith to God-ward is spread abroad; so that we need not to speak any thing" (1 Thessalonians 1:8).

SOME EXAMPLES IN EARLY HISTORY

Here are the thoughts of one historian:

> It is a remarkable fact that after the days of the Apostles no names of great missionaries are mentioned till the opening of the middle ages. . . . There were no missionary societies, no missionary institutions, no organized efforts in the ante-Nicene age; and yet in less than 300 years from the death of St. John the whole population of the Roman empire which then represented the civilized world was nominally Christianized.
>
> To understand this astonishing fact, we must remember that the foundation was laid strong and deep by the apostles themselves. . . .
>
> Christianity once established was its own best missionary. . . . And while there were no professional missionaries devoting their whole life to this specific work, every congregation was a missionary society, and every Christian believer a missionary, inflamed by the love of Christ to convert his fellow-men. . . . Justin Martyr was converted by a venerable old man whom he met walking on the shore of the sea. . . . Celsus scoffingly remarks that fullers and workers in wool and leather, rustic and ignorant persons, were the most zealous propagators of Christianity, and brought it first

to women and children. Women and slaves introduced it into the home-circle. . . . Origen informs us that the city churches sent their missionaries to the villages. . . . Every Christian told his neighbor, the laborer to his fellow-laborer, the slave to his fellow-slave, the servant to his master and mistress, the story of his conversion, as a mariner tells the story of the rescue from shipwreck.[11]

Eusebius, a Greek Christian historian living in the third and fourth centuries, wrote of the evangelistic activity prevalent around the time of Polycarp, a second-century bishop.

Many others were well known at the time, belonging to the first stage in the apostolic succession. These earnest disciples of great men built on the foundations of the churches everywhere laid by the apostles, spreading the message still further and sowing the saving seed of the Kingdom of Heaven far and wide through the entire world. Very many of the disciples of the time, their hearts smitten by the word of God with an ardent passion . . . fulfilled the Saviour's command by distributing their possessions among the needy; then, leaving their homes behind, they carried out the work of evangelists, ambitious to preach to those who had never yet heard the message of

---

[11] Philip Schaff, *History of the Christian Church*, 2:20–21.

faith. . . . Staying only to lay the foundations of the faith in one foreign place or another, appoint others as pastors, and entrust to them the tending of those newly brought in, they set off again for other lands and peoples with the grace and cooperation of God.[12]

Justin Martyr wrote these words around the year A.D.160:

"His blood I will require at your hand. But if you warn him, you will be innocent." For this reason, out of fear, we are very earnest in desiring to witness according to the Scriptures —but not from love of money, of glory, or of pleasure.[13]

Origen, a third-century Christian, wrote the following:

We *do* desire to instruct all men in the word of God, so as to give to young men the exhortations that are appropriate to them. . . . And those among us who are the ambassadors of Christianity sufficiently declare that they are "debtors to Greeks and barbarians, to wise men and fools." . . . There are some who are capable of receiving nothing more than an exhortation to believe. To these, that is all we address. However, we approach others, to the extent possible, in the way of demonstration by means of questions and answers. . . .

---

[12] Eusebius, *The History of the Church*, 100.
[13] David Bercot, ed., *A Dictionary of Early Christian Beliefs*, 260.

Christians do not neglect (as far as in them lies)
to take steps to disseminate their doctrine
throughout the whole world. Accordingly,
some of them have made it their business to
travel not only through cities, but even to
villages and rural houses in order to make
converts to God. And no one would claim that
they did this for the sake of gain.[14]

Philip Schaff, in his extensive writings about the church,
quoted Tertullian:

Every Christian . . . both finds out God and
manifests him, though . . . it is not easy to
discover the Creator, and difficult when He is
found to make Him known to all.[15]

What zeal! The early Christians did not question the
application of Christ's last commission. They read the New
Testament and, in childlike faith, put it into action. They told
the good news to whomever they met. Most likely, those
who traveled as evangelists did not appoint themselves, but
were sent by their congregations, according to Romans
10:15.

Certainly, we weren't there to witness this phase of
history; we can only go by what historians have preserved
on paper. We cannot be certain that every individual was a
zealous missionary or that every congregation was
evangelistic. Nevertheless, the early church seems to have
had commendable evangelistic zeal. This is understandable,

[14] Ibid., 260–261.
[15] Schaff, *History*, 2:20.

since they were not far removed from the influence of the Savior and the apostles. Instead of fulfilling Christ's commission completely, the apostles had simply laid the groundwork for further evangelistic activity.

Into the Constantinian Era

Throughout the first three centuries after Christ, Christianity was not a tolerable religion. It is believed that ten waves of persecution took place during the first three hundred years of the Christian era.[16]

At the beginning of the fourth century, the political climate changed. The Roman emperor Constantine legalized Christianity, proclaiming it as the official religion of the state church. Eventually, Christianity was not determined by whether a person recognized his sinful nature and experienced a heart conversion. Rather, it was determined by who lived in a certain geographical region.

How did this change affect the true Christians? Since everyone within a certain geographical area was considered a Christian, no longer did it make sense to evangelize. Moreover, the few Christians who acknowledged the separation of church and state were marked as heretics.

If the Romans had suppressed outreach before, the Constantinian movement struck the final blow. In his book *The Reformers and Their Stepchildren*, Leonard Verduin wrote,

> Here we have the beginnings of the notion,
> which reigned supreme in the minds of men all
> through medieval times, that part way into the

---

[16] Ben Giesbrecht, *The Enduring Church*, 26–27.

Christian era a change was intended by the King of the Church himself—a change whereby the world of apostolic times would become obsolete. This change was identified with the Constantinian innovation. This idea set forth by Augustine controlled the thought and the theology of European man all through medieval times. It led to all sorts of theological absurdities—as, for example, that the Great Commission was intended for the pre-Constantinian era and had with the Constantinian change been fulfilled.[17]

As will be further discussed in Chapter 7, many plain churches assume Christ's last commission was only meant for the apostles. The nominal Christians after the time of Constantine seem to have assumed that Christ's last commission was intended for more than just the apostles, but only for Christians before the Constantinian era. Do you see the irony here?

Nevertheless, mission work continued, but it became more institutionalized. Philip Schaff wrote,

> The medieval Christianization was a wholesale conversion, or a conversion of nations under the command of their leaders. It was carried on not only by missionaries and by spiritual means, but also by political influence . . . and in some cases . . . by military force. It was a conversion not to the primary Christianity of

---

[17] Leonard Verduin, *The Reformers and Their Stepchildren*, 66.

inspired apostles, as laid down in the New
Testament, but to the secondary Christianity of
ecclesiastical tradition, as taught by the fathers,
monks and popes. . . .

The missionaries of the middle ages were
nearly all monks. They were generally men of
limited education and narrow views, but
devoted zeal and heroic self-denial.[18]

In his book *The Pilgrim Church*, E.H. Broadbent wrote of
misguided mission efforts throughout medieval times.

The errors . . . which prevailed in the professing
churches were reflected in their missionary
work. There was no longer the simple
preaching of Christ and founding of churches
as in the early days, but . . . also insistence on
ritual and legal observances; and when kings
came to confess Christianity, the principle of
Church and State led to the forcible outward
conversion of multitudes of their subjects to the
new State religion. Instead of churches being
founded in different towns and countries . . . as
in apostolic days, all were drawn into one of the
great organizations which had its center in
Rome or Constantinople or elsewhere.[19]

Constantine reasoned that many more people would
become attracted to Christianity if church buildings would

---

[18] Schaff, *History*, 4:18–19.
[19] E.H. Broadbent, *The Pilgrim Church*, 56.

be built more lavishly. At great expense, new church buildings rivaled the grandeur of pagan temples. Many of these buildings included fountains, marble floors, and vaulted ceilings. In this way, unbelievers found it difficult to walk past without being tempted to stop in and view the impressive architecture. As a result, thousands of pagans were "converted" to Christianity.[20]

Bright Pockets in Dark Ages

Even though many mission efforts during that era were not Scripturally sound, we do well to view history charitably. Some souls received the knowledge of truth who otherwise would never have, and that includes our own ancestors. As the apostle Paul wrote, "What then? notwithstanding, every way, whether in pretence, or in truth, Christ is preached; and I therein do rejoice, yea, and will rejoice" (Philippians 1:18).

Nevertheless, some bright pockets existed throughout the Dark Ages. Some churches, though labeled as heretical, seemed more Biblical than the state churches. Some zealous individuals existed in nominal churches, such as Saint Patrick. Born in Britain, probably sometime in the late fourth or early fifth century, he was taken captive to Ireland when he was sixteen years old. There he served six years as a slave tending sheep. In a dream, God told Patrick to escape, which he did, only to be taken captive again by a band of sailors. Nevertheless, he arrived home in Britain several months later. Shortly afterward, he had another dream from God, directing him to return to Ireland as a missionary. However,

[20] David Bercot, *Will the Real Heretics Please Stand Up*, 127.

twenty-five years passed before his home church authorized him to go. But God is always on time. Twenty-five years later, the Irish were more receptive to the Gospel.[21]

Another influential missionary was Boniface, who was born around A.D. 680. Although his first attempt was a failure, this only increased his courage. He journeyed to Rome, where Pope Gregory welcomed him and gave him a commission to evangelize central Europe.[22] We have some preserved records of his writings, which illustrate what he taught. He wrote,

> Listen, my brethren, and consider well what you have solemnly renounced in your baptism. You have renounced the devil and all his works. . . . And these are the commandments which you shall keep and fulfil: to love God, whom you profess, with all your heart, all your soul, and all your strength, and to love your neighbor as yourselves. . . . Teach your sons to fear God; teach your whole family to do so. . . . Show hospitality to travelers, visit the sick, take care of widows and orphans, pay your tithes to the church, and do to nobody what you would not have done to yourself. . . . Believe in the advent of Christ, the resurrection of the body, and the judgment of all men. . . . [Remove] all malice and hatred and envy; it is poison to your heart. . . . Keep peace with all, and make peace between those who are at discord. If, with the

---

[21] David Bercot, *Let Me Die In Ireland;* Schaff, *History,* 4:45–46.
[22] Schaff, *History,* 4:92–96.

aid of Christ, you will truly fulfil these
commands, then in this life you can with
confidence approach the altar of God, and in
the next you shall partake of the everlasting
bliss.[23]

The Nestorians also hold a commendable record of
spreading the Gospel in Asia. Yet as Broadbent noted:

Thus love to the Lord and compassion for the
heathen carried these messengers of the Gospel
to the most remote parts, accomplishing
extraordinary journeys, and their word was
accompanied by the saving power of the Holy
Spirit, but at the same time centralization that
had developed caused the increasing departure
of the center from the teachings of Scripture to
be reproduced in new churches, introducing
from the beginning an element of weakness
which bore its fruit in later years.[24]

During the twelfth century, Peter Waldo, a rich merchant,
studied the Bible and was attracted to Jesus' teachings. Over
the next years, he attracted more followers who took the
teachings of Jesus seriously. They read that Christians
should sell their possessions and distribute to the poor, so
that is what they did. They read how Jesus sent His disciples
two by two to witness, and so they did that. On their
missionary journeys, they often traveled as businessmen

[23] *Geschichte der deutschen Predigt in Mittelalter,* 14. Cited in Schaff, *History,* 4:96–98.
[24] Broadbent, *Pilgrim,* 99.

with wares for sale.[25]

Here we have the record of a group similar to the Anabaptists, who endeavored to follow Jesus' teachings no matter what the cost. They read their Bibles and put into practice what they read. They followed the precepts of Christ's teachings with childlike simplicity, and their church flourished during the Dark Ages.

Today we have been affected both positively and negatively by our background and frame of reference. Certainly, we can never escape who we are. And we naturally defend our preferences. But are we truly open to learning different concepts for the advancement of Christ's kingdom?

Of course, in our setting we may not be called to live exactly as others did. But have we perhaps lost sight of some principles because we prefer more lenient applications? On some Scripture passages, we might disagree with other Biblical groups, such as the Waldenses and the early Anabaptists. Yet shouldn't we be learning from the Scriptural points of these groups, rather than discounting them as radical?

Thus far we have explored church history up to the Waldenses of the twelfth and thirteenth centuries. The best part of church history is yet to come. Get ready for some astounding evangelistic evidence in Anabaptist history.

---

[25] Ibid., 121.

The Missing Spoke

Chapter Three

The Anabaptists: Zealous Missionaries or the "Quiet in the Land"?

I t is with misgivings that I write this chapter. To rightly interpret history without biases, both personal and historical, is a challenge. How can we be assured that all our historical sources are accurate? We were not witnesses to these happenings, and we have nothing to go by except what previous historians have written.

We cannot ignore the fact that we are biased. We like to study and interpret history according to our preferences and frame of reference. This is especially so in regard to the history of our forefathers. Instead of studying history to find out what we should learn from them, we would rather conform their history to our beliefs.

When we think of our forefathers, then, what is our impression? Do we visualize them as the "quiet in the land" who obeyed Christ's teachings? Or do we view them as people who faced hatred, opposition, and persecution from the authorities, and who chose to suffer and die rather than deny their faith? We would like to think that the Anabaptist churches in Europe were similar to our plain churches today. In some ways they were. Nevertheless, we may be less comfortable with the fact that many of the early Anabaptists were zealous missionaries who freely spread their doctrines, which provoked wrath from the state churches.

As you read this chapter, please keep two things in mind. First, the Bible, not Anabaptism, is our final authority. Whether or not the Anabaptists were evangelistic should not be our only guide. Our view of evangelism must be based on the New Testament.

Second, this chapter cannot cover everything the Anabaptists believed. My perspective of Anabaptist history might seem unbalanced, since the focus is on their missionary zeal rather than on their beliefs.

Were the Anabaptists Indeed Evangelistic?

The initial Anabaptist movement had many faces. This could be because Anabaptism did not emerge solely at one time or place. The term *Anabaptist* literally means "rebaptizer." The authorities labeled everyone "Anabaptist" who received rebaptism, although technically they had received only one authentic baptism. However, not every Anabaptist group upheld Scriptural doctrines. Some radical movements emerged soon after 1525. The Münster revolt in 1535 is evidence that not all "Anabaptists" were true followers of Christ.

Anabaptism originated on January 21, 1525, when George Blaurock requested that Conrad Grebel baptize him, and George then baptized Felix Manz and Conrad. Others in attendance requested baptism too.

Did this small group then quietly slip back into the routine of daily life? Was the only difference that they now held church services separately from the state church in the canton of Zurich? Was their lifestyle and good example their only witness of what had happened? Did they wait to baptize more converts until seekers knocked on their doors? I am not aware of any record that gives us this impression. The new movement did not remain at Zurich. One historian states that within a week it spread to Zollikon, where the brethren witnessed, baptized, and held communion. At least thirty-five people were baptized.[26]

Another historian also bears witness to the missionary activity.

> Immediately after the formation of the first Anabaptist church, the Brethren began a house-to-house visitation in Zürich and Zollikon. Baptisms were frequent, and the Lord's Supper was observed in the simplest manner upon several occasions. Manz and Blaurock spearheaded the drive for converts in the Zürich area. In the early days of the movement

---

[26] Michael Martin, *Cup and Cross*, 55.

Grebel attempted to carry the Anabaptist message to the leaders of the Reformation in Schaffhausen. Manz and Blaurock, meanwhile, continued their efforts among the farmers and artisans of Zollikon. This division of labor was not rigidly followed. Manz did attempt to witness to Dr. Hofmeister on one occasion, as Hofmeister testified at the trial of 1526.[27]

Such boldness and courage! All this happened in the face of persecution. Although the record of evangelistic activity seems to center around these three leaders, we have no reason to think that other members, having made the commitment to be baptized, did not also witness boldly whenever possible. Since the Anabaptists had been only recently delivered from the legalistic bondage of the Roman Catholic Church, they naturally had compassion toward those who were still in bondage, and desired that they also would find true freedom.

Enemies Testify to Anabaptist Evangelistic Zeal

The enemies of the first Anabaptists passed down some evidence of the evangelistic zeal of the new group. In June 1525, Ulrich Zwingli, the prominent reformer with whom Blaurock, Manz, and Grebel had parted ways, published a tract against the Anabaptists' "unauthorized" outreach:

Therefore those who pretend to be apostles or prophets do not, in expositing the Scripture, act according to the practice of the apostles. They

---

[27] William R. Estep, *The Anabaptist Story*, 45–46.

do not stay in their own churches but run to other churches and speak there without the prophets. And whereas they use this passage by Paul to prove that they may also interrupt by speaking from Scripture, they refuse to be interrupted themselves. . . .

. . . At Jerusalem there were thousands of believers, but there were no more than twelve apostles. Here all of them are apostles. I believe there are more apostles than believers! If one has attended a German school and has learned to spell, he appears in public and spells it out to the congregation.[28]

Sebastian Franck, another opponent of the Anabaptists, testified in 1531 to their rapid spread.

The Anabaptists spread so rapidly that their teaching soon covered, as it were, the land. They soon gained a large following, and baptized many thousands, drawing to themselves many sincere souls who had a zeal for God. . . . They increased so rapidly that the world feared an uprising by them, though I have learned that this fear had no justification whatsoever. They were persecuted with great tyranny, being imprisoned, branded, tortured, and executed by fire, water, and the sword. . . .

---

[28] Ulrich Zwingli, *Concerning the Office of Preaching,* June 3, 1525. Cited in Martin, *Cup and Cross,* 259.

They died as martyrs, patiently, and humbly endured all persecution.[29]

More Evidence According to Written History

The Anabaptists made no secret of their belief in evangelizing. In the first year of the Anabaptist movement, one of the converts proclaimed to Ulrich Zwingli and Leo Jüd, "If you were as evangelical as you think you are, you would obey the Gospel and go out as emissaries of God, to preach the Word of God and return the erring to the right way."[30]

Indeed, if the movement had not spread rapidly in those first years, it might well have been extinguished. But some sources state that for every Anabaptist executed, several others replaced him. One executor is thought to have said, "The more rebaptizers I kill the greater their numbers!"[31]

Conrad Grebel died from a plague about eighteen months after the birth of the Anabaptist movement. Felix Manz was drowned soon afterward, while George Blaurock was banished and eventually burned at the stake. But the Anabaptist movement was far from dying out. Members seem to have continued their mission work in the course of their daily lives.

Some deliberate planning was also done. On August 20, 1527, in Augsburg, Germany, a meeting was held to discuss some issues and to determine a strategic program for outreach. About sixty men were appointed in groups of two

---

[29] John Horsch, *Mennonites in Europe*, 293.
[30] Verduin, *Reformers*, 269.
[31] Benuel Blank, *Resurrection to Reformation and Beyond*, 156.

and three to travel throughout the German-speaking regions of Europe. This historic meeting has since been called the Martyrs' Synod because many of the men who attended the meeting were later martyred for their faith. Their mission, however, was not in vain.[32] It was so effective that opponents claimed the evangelists carried flasks of magic water or a potion to cast spells on their audiences. They thought this was what influenced people to convert to Anabaptism and change so drastically.

Menno Simons, a prominent Dutch Anabaptist leader, also felt a burden that every soul might come to the true faith and experience salvation. He wrote the following:

> We desire with ardent hearts, even at the cost of life and blood, that the holy gospel of Jesus Christ and his apostles, which alone is the true doctrine, and will remain so until Jesus Christ will reappear in the clouds, may be taught and preached through all the world, as the Lord Jesus Christ commanded his disciples at the last moments while he was on earth.[33]
>
> . . . This is my only joy and the desire of my heart, that I may extend the borders of the kingdom of God, publish the truth, reprove sin, teach righteousness, feed the hungry with the word of the Lord, lead the stray sheep into the right path, and win many souls to the Lord

---

[32] David G. Burkholder, *Distinctive Beliefs of the Anabaptists*, 38–39; Martin, *Cup and Cross*, 258; Theron Schlabach, *Gospel Versus Gospel*, 26.

[33] *Menno Simons, Complete Works*, pt. 2:243.

through his Spirit, power, and grace.[34]

. . . Therefore we would teach, proclaim and
imprint on the hearts of all mankind, to the best
of our ability, this manifest grace of his great
love toward us, that they may enjoy with us the
same joy and renewal of spirit, and know and
taste with all saints how sweet, good and kind
the Lord is to whom we have turned.

We preach, therefore, as much as is in our
power, both day and night, in houses and in the
open air, in forests and in wildernesses, hither
and thither, in this and in foreign lands, in
prisons and in dungeons, in water and in fire,
on the scaffold and on the wheel, before lords
and princes, orally and by writings at the risk of
possessions and blood, life and death; as we
have done these many years.[35]

Wolfgang Vogel, an Anabaptist executed in 1527, wrote,

Christianity is neither an affair of dark alleys
nor a smuggler's ware. Therefore, dear
brethren, do not keep it to yourselves but do as
the dear apostles did who publicly declared
that one must obey God rather than man.[36]

Matthias Servaes wrote a number of letters to his
brethren while he was in prison in 1565. In one letter he

---

[34] Ibid., pt. 1:75.
[35] Ibid., pt. 2:10.
[36] Robert Friedmann, *Mennonite Piety Through the Centuries*, 27.

52

expressed his concern for lost souls.

> And be also not slothful in seeking men's souls;
> wherever you have some hope, there go. Say,
> not: "It will be labor lost." Put your hand to the
> plow first, in the fear of the Lord, and ask Him
> to give the blessing; but you do the planting
> and watering. Pray the Lord to give the
> increase. And if then your endeavors are
> unsuccessful, you are free. For I have often felt
> accused, that we have not much more sought
> men's souls, to the praise of the Lord.[37]

Hutterite Missionary Zeal

Among the Anabaptists, the Hutterites seem to hold the record for being the most zealous in evangelizing. They experienced longer periods of peace in Moravia than did the Anabaptists in other regions, except for the Netherlands. Many Swiss brethren in Switzerland and south Germany joined the Hutterite movement. The Hutterites were noted for sending evangelists to other regions in Europe, who returned with converts interested in moving to their colonies. This was a risky venture. Many converts enroute to Moravia were arrested by authorities and executed. As in the case of the resulting missionary dispersion from the 1527 "Martyrs' Synod", many Hutterite missionaries never returned; some historians estimate as many as eighty percent.[38]

---

[37] Thieleman J. van Braght, *Martyrs Mirror,* 690.
[38] Martin, *Cup and Cross,* 191; Estep, *Story,* 134; John Hofer, *History of the Hutterites,* 30.

A Catholic historian named Josef Beck noted,

> Every year, usually after the day of co-
> memoration (breaking of bread), several were
> solemnly sent forth "to gather sheep to the
> Lord," or as their opponents expressed, "to fish
> for people." Their mission was dangerous,
> mostly ending with dungeon and death.[39]

The council in Bern, Switzerland, noticed the Hutterite
missionary activity. Government decrees hindered
emigration to Moravia. Those who migrated to Moravia lost
their citizenship and could not move back to Switzerland.

Claus Felbinger, a Hutterite missionary, said,

> We have been asked by sundry people why we
> have come into the prince's land, and draw
> people away. My answer is, we do not go only
> into this land, but into all lands, wherever our
> language is known, for where God opens a
> door for us and shows us zealous hearts that
> truly seek Him . . . there we go, for we have
> divine cause to do so.[40]

Others described this as well:

> The witnesses to the truth who were sent forth
> by the brotherhood, gave testimony earnestly
> and steadfastly to the Word of the Lord, by
> their life and work, by word and deed. They

---

[39] Cited in Ernst Müller, *History of the Bernese Anabaptists*, 105.
[40] Estep, *Story*, 257.

spoke with power of the kingdom of God, showing that all men must repent, be converted, and turn to God from the vanity of this world and its unrighteousness, from a sinful, vile, and wanton life. To all such work God gave His blessing, so that it was carried on with joy.

The Christian mission work is carried on among us according to the command of Christ: "As my Father hath sent me, even so send I you," and again: "I have chosen you and ordained you, that ye should go forth and bring fruit." Accordingly, ministers of the Gospel and their assistants are annually sent forth into the various countries to those who desire to amend their lives and are asking for the truth. Such are brought to the brotherhood in Moravia, in spite of hangman and headsman, notwithstanding the fact that many were apprehended while on their way to Moravia and suffered martyrdom. [41]

Anabaptist Nicknames

Another evidence of Anabaptist evangelistic zeal was the nicknames their opponents called them. In his book *The Reformers and Their Stepchildren,* Leonard Verduin gives some examples. They were called *Schwärmer,* which probably meant fanatics, dreamers, or visionaries. This word is related to our English word *swarm.* Another term, *Schleicher,* is related to our Pennsylvania German word *schlichtig,*

---

[41] Cited in Horsch, *Mennonites,* 315–316.

which means "sly" or "stealthy." They were called *Truands,* a word related to our English word *truant,* one who does not remain in his expected place. They were called *Gyrovagi,* meaning "wanderers in circles." *Gartenbrüder* meant "wandering brethren." The Anabaptists were also called *Leufer,* which meant "one who walks or runs." That term was used to stigmatize the Anabaptists in their mission endeavors.[42]

Even to their deaths, the Anabaptists' witness continued. One historian noted, "So powerful was the Anabaptist witness at the time of execution, that they were increasingly carried on in secret, or the martyrs were gagged."[43] Michael Sattler's tongue was cut out. Jacob Hutter had a gag stuffed into his mouth. Sometimes a martyr's tongue was clamped with a tongue screw.

The quotes above show us that the Anabaptists did not consider Christ's last commission binding on the apostles alone. Rather, awareness of their part in fulfilling this commission grew as they studied the Bible and, in simple faith and obedience, applied it to their own lives.

The Protestant reformers, however, did not spread the Gospel in the same way as the Anabaptists did. They believed that Christ's last commission only applied to the apostles. Justus Menius, a Lutheran opponent of the Anabaptists, wrote,

> The Apostles made disposition not only for
> themselves but also left behind them—through
> their disciples and in their writings, teachings,

---

[42] Verduin, *Reformers,* 263, 266.
[43] Cornelius Dyck, *An Introduction to Mennonite History,* 112.

and examples—[instruction] as to how the Church should act in calling servants of the Gospel: namely, that the servant of the Gospel does not travel here and there about the land— in one church today, another tomorrow; preaching one time white, another time black. But one servant steadily watches over his assigned church with true industry and remains with it, leaving other churches untroubled and in peace. Each church has thereby its own constituted servant and excludes strange unappointed spiritual gypsies.[44]

How Twentieth Century Historians Distorted Anabaptist History

Joseph Stoll, an Amish authority on Anabaptist history, explains how the missionary emphasis of the early Anabaptists has been used to encourage many Plain People to gradually accept the modern mission emphasis. He writes,

For years historians had given [the Anabaptists] a very unflattering report. They had labeled as the black sheep of the Reformation . . . But that all began to change. The Anabaptists were at last recognized as champions and pioneers of the free church concept. During the 1940s, too, historians began

---

[44] Cited in Franklin H. Littell, *The Anabaptist View of the Church*, 114–115.

to exalt the Anabaptists as pioneers in missions."[45]

During the 1940s a scholar named Franklin H. Littell did more research and made even stronger statements. Stoll writes of Littell:

> Few historical articles have had as great an impact on the Mennonite church as Littell's chapter on missions. It has been quoted again and again, and reference to his research appears in virtually every major study on Mennonite missions since then. As far as I knew when I began this article, his scholarship had never been challenged. So there was reason to tremble before suggesting that in some respects Littell has not only overstated his case but has also distorted the historical facts.[46]

Littell wrote a whole chapter on the Anabaptist view of Christ's last commission. Although much of the chapter may be accurate, I believe Stoll is right to question some parts. For example, Littell stated that Christ's last commission was central to the Anabaptists' testimony. He wrote,

> According to Anabaptist understanding of right faith, the Great Commission was fundamental to individual witness and to the ordered community of believers as well. The proof text appeared repeatedly in Anabaptist sermons

---

[45] Joseph Stoll, *The Church and Mission Work*, 15–16.
[46] Ibid., 17.

and apologetic writing. Confessions of faith and court testimonies give it a central place.[47]

It is true that Christ's last commission found a central place among the Anabaptists and was frequently quoted. But the Anabaptists were not necessarily using it to show that Christ intended His last commission for the church in every age. The real issue was believer's baptism. The Anabaptists quoted these verses to prove that believing and repentance must precede baptism.

Nevertheless, we should not assume that the Anabaptists ignored the first part of the command. Why would they have quoted these verses to defend believer's baptism if they had considered these passages to be solely intended for the apostles?

According to James C. Juhnke, the first Americanized study of Anabaptist/Mennonite history was C. Henry Smith's book *The Mennonites of America*. Anabaptists were evaluated in terms of American Protestantism, Jeffersonian democracy, and social Darwinism. Smith believed that the genius of the Mennonites was akin to the best and most glorious features of America: individuality and the freedom of conscience. He stated that the Anabaptists were intensely individualistic. They suffered persecution because they were ahead of their times.[48]

Another twentieth-century Mennonite historian, Theron Schlabach, wrote,

---

[47] Littell, *Anabaptist View*, 111.
[48] C. Henry Smith, *The Mennonites of America*. Cited in James C. Juhnke, *Vision, Doctrine, War*, 173–174.

Time after time advocates of mission pointed to Anabaptists' missionary zeal.

Yet even religiously the activists were in some ways becoming less "Mennonite" and more like North Americans in general. The Mennonite Church's quickening was hardly an Anabaptist revival and certainly not a "recovery of the Anabaptist vision." . . .

The fact was, when mission-minded Mennonites in the late years of the nineteenth century pointed to Menno and other Anabaptists as examples, they often seemed to be making the Anabaptists into modern-style missionaries rather than to be asking how the Anabaptists had gone about communicating gospel.[49]

What Schlabach said here seems true. Some historians have indeed slanted Anabaptist history to conform to their bias. Modern Mennonite historians have not been fair to their forefathers. The Anabaptists arrived at their conclusions and engaged in evangelism because of a conscientious adherence to the Bible. Nineteenth- and twentieth-century historians twisted Anabaptist motives.

Liberal Mennonite historians tried to prove that the Anabaptists were evangelistic, to justify their missions theology and methodology. Could Old Order historians be as guilty of distortion as the liberals? Do we study history to

---

[49] Schlabach, **Gospel**, page 44-45.

prove that the Anabaptists were never mission-minded?

Yes, But What about Dirk Philips' Writings?

Dirk Philips was a prominent Dutch Anabaptist leader and coworker of Menno Simons. From what we gather from Dirk's writing, he seemed to agree with the reformers that Christ's last commission only applied to the apostles. Dirk wrote the following:

> The apostles were chosen and sent by Christ to preach the gospel to every creature, and to be witnesses for Christ unto the ends of the earth. Hence God dealt wonderfully with them; but he does not deal thus with all teachers, for they are not like the great apostles; neither does God propose to accomplish through all teachers what he accomplished through the apostles; and therefore he has not imposed upon all teachers what he imposed upon the apostles.
>
> The apostles were commanded by the Lord to preach the gospel to every creature, which, by the grace of God, they did. If this were to be followed out, then the teachers now would have to preach not only to the Christians as mentioned, but also to the Jews, Turks, and all the heathen. But Paul declares to the teachers and bishops of the church that they shall take heed unto themselves, and to all the flock, over the which the Holy Ghost had made them overseers. On the day of Pentecost the apostles

spake with tongues of fire, and everyone understood them. This never came to pass before that time, nor has it come to pass since. God also wonderfully delivered the apostles out of prison. Now let him who would say that teachers should preach openly as Christ and his apostles did, remember that Christ could deliver himself from the hands of his enemies whenever he wished, and that God dealt miraculously with his apostles.[50]

These quotes from Dirk Philips seem to show that he did not believe in evangelistic outreach. Before we make any conclusions, we must consider several factors. First, Dirk Philips' writings remind us that no Anabaptist writing should take precedence over the inspired Word of God. The Anabaptist writings, for or against evangelism, are only valuable as they point us back to the Scriptures.

Second, Philips was writing to refute the opponents of Anabaptism, who accused the Anabaptists of not preaching openly. Earlier in his article, Dirk explained why signs, miracles, and wonders were used in the New Testament era, but no longer in the current age. Perhaps some opponents were accusing the Dutch Anabaptists of not being authorized to evangelize, since they could not perform miracles. At any rate, it seems that Dirk was defending, not criticizing, the evangelistic activity of his Christian brethren.

Indeed, had Dirk opposed his coworkers, Menno Simons and Leonard Bouwens, concerning evangelistic outreach, a

---

[50] Dirk Philips, *Enchiridion, or Handbook of the Christian Doctrine and Religion*, 211–212.

split would probably have resulted among the Dutch Anabaptists. During his ministry, Leonard Bouwens baptized more than ten thousand people.[51] Many of these applicants were won as a result of evangelistic efforts of many Dutch Anabaptists. These Mennonites held to their theological beliefs and expelled those who did not agree with them; it seems doubtful that Philips and Bouwens would have maintained sharply different views.

In light of the above factors, it is hardly fair to assume that Dirk was completely against any form of mission outreach. Dirk's full meaning and his goals for writing are not clear. It is possible that in answering the accusations of his opponents, he contradicted himself. His strong view that it was right for Christians to hide to decrease the risk of persecution was probably controversial. Many other Anabaptists seemed bolder and faced death as a result.

Why Did the Anabaptist Outreach Vision Die?

As zealous as the Anabaptists were in sharing their faith at the beginning of the Anabaptist movement, it eventually died out. Even the Hutterites lost it. How did it happen, and why?

Because we weren't eyewitnesses of that era, we do not have all the details. Some historians say that intense persecution drove many Anabaptists to hide in caves in the mountains or to flee to more isolated regions. Thus, the brutality of the opposition may eventually have led the Anabaptists to become the "quiet in the land," content merely to pass on the faith to their children while hoping

---

[51] Horsch, *Mennonites,* 316.

- that their example would still be effective. However, persecution does not seem to have been the main factor.

After the Thirty Years' War (1618–48) had devastated the Palatinate, the governor hoped to rebuild the land and economy. He invited Protestants, Catholics, and Anabaptists to settle the area. Although the Reformed Church (the state church) succeeded in having Anabaptist meetings outlawed in 1661, that ruling was changed by 1664. The Anabaptists were again allowed to have meetings, but they were not allowed to invite non-Anabaptists. Apparently, the Anabaptists gladly accepted this ruling, which shows a drift in their evangelistic vision.[52]

Another factor could be that they were not completely successful in passing on their evangelistic vision to the second and third generations. The evidence for evangelistic zeal seems to come largely from the first generation.

Probably the best explanation I've found as to why the Anabaptist zeal for outreach dwindled is William McGrath's diagram on the sect cycle.[53] This cycle seems to accurately describe the Anabaptist movement from 1525 to the present. Why can't we reverse the sect cycle by going back to number two and becoming a thriving missionary church? Even if it means enduring persecution, couldn't we still stay at number two?

---

[52] Martin, *Cup and Cross*, 103.
[53] William McGrath, *Conservative Anabaptist Theology*, 44.

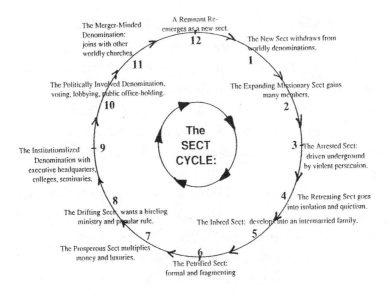

The Merger-Minded Denomination: joins with other worldly churches

11

A Remnant Re-emerges as a new sect.

12

The New Sect withdraws from worldly denominations.

1

The Politically Involved Denomination, voting, lobbying, public office-holding.

10

The Expanding Missionary Sect gains many members.

2

The Institutionalized Denomination with executive headquarters, colleges, seminaries.

9

The SECT CYCLE:

3 The Arrested Sect: driven underground by violent persecution.

8

The Drifting Sect wants a hireling ministry and popular rule.

7

4 The Retreating Sect goes into isolation and quietism.

The Inbred Sect: develops into an intermarried family.

5

The Prosperous Sect multiplies money and luxuries.

6

The Petrified Sect: formal and fragmenting

Pietism's Effect on Anabaptist Zeal

McGrath's sect cycle, however, does not fully explain why Anabaptist missionary zeal eventually phased out. During the seventeenth century, a new movement emerged within the Reformed state churches after some members became dissatisfied with the formality in the state church. They wanted a deeper experience of a relationship with God. These people became known as Pietists because they represented cells of piety in a time when many members of the state church seemed hopelessly corrupt. These Pietists often met with other like-minded people to study the Bible and to share religious experiences. Anabaptism differed from Pietism in its application of a New Testament believers' church. The Anabaptists taught that a strict separation from the state churches was necessary to maintain the vision of a

65

pure New Testament Church. As a result, they faced arrest, persecution, harassment, and death.

Pietism, on the other hand, provided an escape from the trials and hurdles the Anabaptists faced. Since the Pietists still kept their membership within the state church, they did not face persecution as did the Anabaptists. Thus they avoided conflict while basking in the joy of their religious experience.

Why has Pietism been a threat to Anabaptist churches? Because Pietism has never formed a true church based on New Testament principles. When the Anabaptist vision dwindled, Pietism increased. The so-called spirituality of the Pietists seemed more attractive to Christians than the formal church life of the Anabaptists. We don't know how many of the subsequent generations of Anabaptists lost their children to this influence. The Pietist mentality seemed to be, "Why join the Anabaptists when you can have a sweet Christian experience right where you are and not even have to face persecution?"

Many Pietists became "true-hearted" people, members in the state churches who rendered assistance to the persecuted Anabaptists. The fate of the true-hearted was one of the controversies in the Amish-Mennonite confrontation in 1693. Since some of the Anabaptists were ready to consider the true-hearted as brothers and sisters, their zeal for evangelizing was dampened. Pietism thus seemed responsible for warping the original Anabaptist concept of evangelism.

Pietism still threatens the Anabaptist brotherhood model

today. Although a personal conversion experience is not to be downplayed, Pietism, by its very nature, claims spirituality while promoting a spirit of individualism. On the other hand, if Satan cannot succeed in attacking us from one angle, he will try another. Pietism has many faces. We might successfully keep one form from taking root, yet miss another form. If Pietism was responsible for dampening Anabaptist zeal for evangelism, that threat is still real today. We value our own brotherhood highly. But possibly we don't quite perceive the value of helping others find what we have. We tend to think it is not necessary or practical to evangelize in our time because others can become Christians without joining our churches. Furthermore, they would not be willing to give themselves up to our lifestyle, language, and culture. Why bother?

Such reasoning is Pietism smacking us in the face. The Pietists avoided conflict by remaining in the state churches. Later generations of Anabaptists lessened their conflict with the authorities by becoming the "quiet in the land." We too can avoid conflict by keeping quiet. But is that what God wants of us?

Are We Willing to Risk Our Lives?

The early Anabaptists were zealous in spreading their faith. They valued other people's souls more highly than their own lives. Had they kept quiet, they would have significantly lessened the risk of arrest. Already in 1533 some Swiss cantons agreed to leave the Anabaptists unmolested if they agreed to keep their faith to themselves.[54]

---

[54] Horsch, *Mennonites,* 102–103; Blank, *Resurrection,* 155.

Notice the difference in how the early and later Anabaptists responded to similar decrees. In spite of persecution, the early Anabaptist movement kept on spreading. How was that possible? The faith and courage of the martyrs brought converts into the Anabaptist churches by the thousands. The state churches seemed dead in formalism. Many believers were thus attracted to Anabaptist congregations in spite of the risk of arrest, imprisonment, banishment, torture, or death.

We don't experience persecution like the Anabaptists did in Europe. One reason is that we live in a more tolerant setting. Might another reason be that we don't quite have the faith, conviction, boldness, courage, and zeal that the early Anabaptists had? Would we see an increase of persecution in America if we became active witnesses for Christ? Even if the government continued to grant protection, would we be willing to suffer violence and scorn from unbelievers who find our message offensive? Would we consider it joy to be counted worthy to suffer for Christ's sake? Refusing to evangelize because of possibly offending unbelievers and nominal Christians seems like a poor excuse in light of early Anabaptist history.

In summary, the Anabaptists were not perfect. We cannot pursue certain mission strategies just because that is how the Anabaptists did it. We do not know how the church body fared when ordained leaders and lay members went on missionary journeys or were martyred. The death of a leader could easily have meant the end of a congregation, although the Anabaptists had a commendable record of ordaining new leaders when existing leaders were martyred.

Some early Anabaptists used methods that we would be slow to endorse. George Blaurock is known to have entered into a state-church meetinghouse and interrupted the speaker.[55] One historian acknowledged that George Blaurock, through his radical methods, could have turned off some who were otherwise in sympathy with the Anabaptist movement.[56]

No doubt some of these early Anabaptists made mistakes that they later regretted. They had their disputes on some issues. But in spite of their imperfections, God used them to extend His kingdom.

"For other foundation can no man lay than that is laid, which is Jesus Christ" (1 Corinthians 3:11). This was the foundation on which the Anabaptists endeavored to build. Although the era of European Anabaptism and its strengths and failures is past, it is up to us to build today on the only sure foundation.

---

[55] Donald Martin, *Joy in Submission,* 20; Estep, S*tory,* 50; Broadbent, *The Pilgrim Church,*
[56] Estep, *Story,* 51.

The Missing Spoke

Chapter Four

Becoming Effective Fishermen

T he great Teacher of Galilee stood by the Lake of Gennesaret. Searching for a secluded place from the pressing throng, He bade Simon Peter, who was cleaning his fishing nets, to enter the boat and thrust it from the land. Peter obeyed and then sat down to listen to the soul-stirring message the Prophet was delivering from the boat to the people flocked by the seashore.

After Jesus had completed His sermon, He turned to Peter and said, "Launch out into the deep, and let down your nets for a catch."

Peter sighed. "Master, we have toiled all night and have caught nothing. However, since you command it, I will let down the net."

So Peter cast his net into the sea. Scarcely was the net submerged when he felt its handle bulging. Immediately Peter knew he could not manage this exceptional catch of fish alone, so he beckoned to his partners, James and John, to come and help. The three of them managed to pull the full net onto both of the boats. The boats filled up, threatening to sink.

Astonished at his extreme catch of fish, and realizing that it was because he had simply obeyed Jesus' instructions, Peter felt humbled. Falling down at Jesus' knees, he said, "Depart from me, for I am a sinful man, O Lord."

And Jesus replied, "Don't be afraid; from now on you will catch men." As soon as Peter and his partners had landed their boats, they forsook all and followed Him.[57]

The disciples had been unsuccessful in their fishing before Jesus arrived on the scene. Jesus used this happening as an object lesson to illustrate that by following Him, they would be successful also in fishing for the souls of men. Here is a spiritual lesson: Even man's best intentions and efforts in evangelizing are as futile as the disciples' fishing during the night. But once we commit ourselves to following Jesus, He will direct us where to cast our nets to fish for the souls of men. For us, the results might not be manifest until eternity.

God's Role Versus Man's Role in Outreach

In the beginning, God created an orderly and perfect world. After our first ancestors sinned, God promised to send a Redeemer to bruise the head of the wily serpent. God showed His love by reaching out to man in spite of man's sinfulness.

Jesus came to earth to carry on the ministry of His Father.

---

[57] Luke 5:1–11.

This meant reaching out to the Jews and, in the course of time, to the Gentiles.

Jesus promised His disciples that they would receive His Spirit. He earnestly desired that His followers would be one. We are His ambassadors, so this ultimately becomes our desire: to reach out to others with the Gospel of the kingdom so that they too can be one in Christ Jesus.

Jesus said, "I am come to send fire on the earth; and what will I, if it be already kindled?" (Luke 12:49). This fire is a type of the Holy Spirit directing the believer, purging the dross and purifying the soul. It is God's nature to warn and rebuke those living in sin. The Holy Spirit, this fire burning within us, will also constrain us to warn those who are abiding in Satan's camp; and He will reveal to us when it would be best to forbear.

What Jeremiah Discovered

God appointed Jeremiah to prophesy to Israel of the impending destruction of their nation. One of the people to whom Jeremiah prophesied was Pashur, the chief governor in the house of the Lord.[58] Rather than humbling himself and repenting of his sins, Pashur took the carnal approach. He gave in to the temptation to torment the prophet. Pashur struck Jeremiah and bound him in stocks. The next day when he released Jeremiah, the prophet told him, "The LORD hath not called thy name Pashur, but Magor-missabib. For thus saith the LORD, Behold, I will make thee a terror to thyself, and to all thy friends: and they shall fall by the sword of their enemies, and thine eyes shall behold it: and I

---

[58] Jeremiah 20:1.

will give all Judah into the hand of the king of Babylon, and he shall carry them captive into Babylon, and shall slay them with the sword" (Jeremiah 20:3–4).

Obviously, Jeremiah's message was not popular. Because of his warnings to Judah, his own people hated him. As a result of this reaction from Pashur, Jeremiah was tempted to compromise his prophetic role. "Then I said, I will not make mention of him, nor speak any more in his name. But his word was in mine heart as a burning fire shut up in my bones, and I was weary with forbearing, and I could not stay" (Jeremiah 20:9). Jeremiah discovered that he could not ignore the warnings he was to give to his people.

This happened in an era when God sent His Spirit only to prophets. We are not prophets in the same sense as Jeremiah. Yet under the New Covenant, God has promised His Holy Spirit to every believer. As a result, the Holy Spirit will sometimes prompt us when He wants us to reach out to others and speak to unbelievers about the hope that is within us.

Fishers of Men—Out of the Heart's Abundance

Jesus said, "Out of the abundance of the heart the mouth speaketh" (Matthew 12:34). If our hearts are filled with carnality, our speech will reflect it. If our hearts are filled with spiritual things, that is what will come forth in our speech. When God gives us a desire to be of use to Him in His kingdom, our lips will want to speak with unbelievers about the condition of their souls.

When Jesus called His disciples, He said, "Follow me, and I will make you fishers of men" (Matthew 4:19). As His disciples, Christ makes us "fishers of men." Would a fisherman find success if he lived a comfortable life on the seashore, valuing his strong nets but never launching out into the deep waters?

We never read that any of these Galilean fishermen went out to fish alone. In fishing for men, Jesus always sent His disciples by twos. Two disciples can more effectively witness than one. Further, we do not want to overlook the fact that even the witness of two will not avail much if we work apart from the direction of the church.

Many individuals have started out to be fishers of men, only to end up drowning in the same water. As a result, some of Christ's disciples advocate being fishers of men by their good examples—staying on the shore, living a comfortable life, and hoping that the "fish" find their way to them. In daily life, we do have opportunities to witness without making the sacrifices some missionaries have to make. However, we must realize that part of the mandate for being fishers of men is to purposefully seek out fish for the Lord, even in the deep, far from our shores.

The same Jesus who calmed the storm on the Galilean Sea can also calm the storms that threaten to sink our ships. We are under His protection if He is our pilot; we do not need to fear that our ships will sink. When Jesus calls us to "launch out into the deep" to fish for the souls of men, we can be sure that He can save our ships from sinking.

"Now then we are ambassadors for Christ, as though God did beseech you by us: we pray you in Christ's stead, be ye reconciled to God" (2 Corinthians 5:20). Since Christ is no longer here bodily, we as His Church are ambassadors in the stead of Christ. "And all things are of God, who hath reconciled us to himself by Jesus Christ, and hath given to us the ministry of reconciliation" (2 Corinthians 5:18).

Christ is still interceding for all men. The Holy Spirit convicts lost souls, and God wants to use His Spirit-filled ambassadors as tools in His hands to reconcile lost souls to Himself. When we are born into God's kingdom, we adopt God's mindset. That includes a desire to lead souls into His kingdom.

Outreach Begins in the Heart

One of the reservations against active evangelism stems from the fear that we could never live consistently enough to apply to ourselves what we are teaching others. Instead, the thinking goes, we should focus on keeping our daily lives consistent with our faith,then we will not be misunderstood. What some fail to consider is that spreading the Gospel of Christ's kingdom motivates us to examine ourselves.

We should realize that if we wait to obey Christ's call until we have reached perfection, we will never fulfill our duty. A minister told me that if he waited to preach until his example and life were perfect, he would never get started. He acknowledged that when he stands up to preach, he is preaching to himself as much as to the rest of the congregation. Being ordained to preach, he said, motivates him to follow Jesus' teachings more fully.

Evangelizing in whatever form is not effective if it is not backed by a consistent example. Coupling evangelism with consistency brings a more powerful witness than one or the other alone. Let us not overlook what the apostle Paul wrote: "What then? Notwithstanding, every way, whether in pretence, or in truth, Christ is preached; and I therein do rejoice, yea, and will rejoice" (Philippians 1:18).

Outreach indeed begins in the heart. The ambassador must first have a relationship with his Lord and Savior. He should continually and thoroughly examine his life to make sure he is reflecting the light entrusted to him as clearly as possible. When he has an opportunity to testify of Christ, he should do all he can to strengthen his witness by his consistent example. The apostle Paul said, "But I keep under my body, and bring it into subjection: lest that by any means, when I have preached to others, I myself should be a castaway" (1 Corinthians 9:27).

The ambassador should have a peaceable relationship with the rest of the church. He should be a supportive pillar in the church. He will not drop the lifestyle and traditions which have been agreed upon by the rest of the congregation, and he will conform his witnessing activity to the guidelines and precepts of his church.

How It Should Not Be Done

How can anyone say wearing plain clothes hinders his witness? Occasionally, someone will approach Plain People with questions because of their dress. Actually, plain clothes and a restricted lifestyle enhance our witness.

While personal witnessing has its place, we must do it under the direction of a godly brotherhood. The world does not understand the concept of Christian brotherhood.

Individualism is prevalent in our society; everyone insists on his own rights. As a result, that mindset has influenced outreach and witnessing. Among some Protestant churches, much emphasis is placed on being a personal witness for Christ.

The church, not the individual, must be central in any evangelistic endeavor. The focus in promoting Christ's kingdom should be on what we can do together. Attempts to evangelize tend to be less fruitful when they are done apart from the direction of the church.

For this reason, I don't think an individual should feel guilty for not beginning new efforts for outreach if he finds himself in a setting where it is not encouraged. Such a person does well to labor on his knees, realizing that God knows the circumstances. Through our earnest seeking, God will eventually open a door when the time is right. In the meantime, such an individual should scrutinize his own life to determine his spiritual growth and faithful use of opportunities that he does have. He must "be ready always to give an answer to every man that asketh [him] a reason of the hope that is in [him] with meekness and fear" (1Peter 3:15). At times, it may be appropriate to steer a conversation to spiritual matters or to inject a comment that makes a person think about God. For myself, I remember times I failed to be the witness I could have been. If I am not willing to commit myself to reaching out in small ways, how can I expect to reach out on a larger scale?

We read in the Bible that whenever God opened doors to service, He chose people who were already faithful in their daily lives. Moses attempted to take matters into his own hands in his zeal to save the Israelites from the Egyptians. However, he took a carnal approach by killing the Egyptian who beat an Israelite. He was forced to flee for his life into the wilderness, and there he found a job tending sheep. Forty years later, Moses had humbled himself. This was the man God was looking for to lead His people out of Egypt. Moses was reluctant; but after much pleading from God, he consented to fulfill his mission.

Likewise, Jesus waited until He was thirty years old to begin His ministry. Before that, He faithfully filled His place in His father's carpenter shop and was a blameless example to all. It was not that conditions did not warrant His active ministry before then. However, the door did not open until He was thirty years old.

It is important to wait for God's timing, especially if we find ourselves in a setting where no direction has been given for outreach. God does not usually lead an individual to take action contrary to the rest of a spiritual brotherhood. This does not mean we are in the wrong if we disagree with others in our congregation. To be able to express a different opinion respectfully characterizes a mature Christian. We must also be willing to face misunderstanding.

Suppose we testify about the strong points of our plain churches and finally attract a seeker to our congregation, but then he discovers that our congregation is divided regarding evangelistic outreach. In such a situation, a seeker would be inclined to feel like a stumbling block.

Evangelizing out of a sense of duty will not accomplish

much. And implementing church-sponsored outreach will not automatically boost spiritual vitality. A carnal person in plain clothes will not necessarily have a change of heart if the church sends him out to witness. A person who thinks he has to evangelize merely because the church says so is no better off than those who think they have to dress and live the way they do because the church says so. Members who lack conviction need teaching and admonition. Outreach in itself is not a magic cure for materialism and complacency; rather, it is the result of a converted and devoted heart.

It will not work to engage in outreach to boost our reputation. To some, it seems glamorous to go to a distant city or foreign country to evangelize. Those who feel that way are likely not finding fulfillment in their daily duties. If we cannot be faithful in lesser duties, how can we expect to be faithful in outreach? To be realistic, evangelistic outreach has its ups and downs. And, like kingdom work, it sometimes feels less rewarding than other pursuits. Many results in evangelistic efforts will not be evident until eternity.

Evangelistic outreach must not be used to cover up disobedience. In some conservative churches, members sometimes deviate from the standards; yet, since they are doing such a noble work of witnessing, leaders hesitate to discipline. Some plain churches have apostatized because of this. Let us never think that the good deeds we do will cancel undesirable deeds. Some things in life cannot be averaged out.

How Should We Be Doing It?

When Jesus gave His parting commission, there was nothing halfway about it. It was a clear mandate that His disciples must teach all nations, or according to Mark, "every creature." The intent of these passages in Matthew, Mark, and Luke cannot be misunderstood. The Gospel is for people of every language, race, culture, tribe, and nation. To our minds, this appears as a daunting assignment. And when we recognize that we cannot get far with this by ourselves, we realize that "the harvest truly is great, but the labourers are few: pray ye therefore the Lord of harvest, that he would send forth labourers into his harvest" (Luke 10:2).

All that we do or say should contribute to the furthering of God's kingdom. When we commit ourselves to serving God, we are dedicating 100 percent of our time and finances to Him. Even our physical labors for our own needs and the needs of our families, and the money we invest to provide for these needs, will all be focused on God's kingdom.

First, let's analyze what we should be doing to become effective witnesses. Our love for God and each other as a church body in a structured community with an accompanying lifestyle is the foremost requirement. If we cannot be a witness in the way we conduct ourselves in daily life, our evangelistic witness will hardly be effective. We must avoid the desire to accumulate earthly wealth. Our daily work must revolve around Christ and His kingdom. Our lifestyle must bear witness that we are living to further Christ's kingdom, not to build our own Amish or Mennonite kingdom. We must maintain lifestyle practices as integral to our faith, but we must not hold them to be the ultimate goal. Our utmost desire should be to glorify God in His kingdom.

One of our foremost responsibilities in being a witness is to "be ready always to give an answer to every man that asketh [us] a reason of the hope that is in [us] with meekness and fear" (1 Peter 3:15). If we are unable to answer in a way that a seeker can understand, it would be better to direct him to a pastor or mature brother who can explain our faith more fully. We fail when we ignore a seeker.

Our contact with people in daily life will provide opportunities to witness. When we are speaking with them about daily business matters, "Let [our] speech be alway with grace, seasoned with salt, that [we] may know how [we] ought to answer every man" (Colossians 4:6). We should speak in such a way that people can see that we have Christ's presence dwelling within us. When their speech is tainted with corruption, we should not respond similarly.

We tend to become like the people with whom we associate. Satan has won a victory if we allow ourselves to be influenced by carnal people, rather than the other way around. If our speech and actions reflect carnality, whether we speak unkindly or pull off a shady business deal, people will lose respect for us and our profession of Christianity. No amount of talking about our faith will convince them differently if our example reveals the opposite.

But if our actions and speech reflect Christ, opportunities will arise to inject comments about God. Greeting a person with "The Lord has given us another beautiful day" might be the key to unlock his heart and to witness about spiritual matters. Too often we neglect our opportunities. A remark about a spiritual point might not open the door for further dialogue, yet we cannot dismiss this strategy. Even if someone does not want to talk further about what we said, he may still think about it. His heart may eventually soften, and he will seek more answers.

How else can we reach out? Should we dispatch a few missionaries to foreign countries? Would we more fully obey this command by sending missionaries to some large American city? Should we support them financially while we continue our comfortable lifestyle, not recognizing the evangelistic duties at our doorstep? The souls of our neighbors down the street are just as precious as those in some far-off country.

Back to Jerusalem

Does that title mean that missionaries are never needed elsewhere? Indeed not. Let us explore some principles integral to a vision of outreach. A good place to start is the first chapter of Acts. This chapter begins with the final instructions Jesus left for His disciples. In verse 4, Jesus commanded that they should not depart from Jerusalem but should wait until they received further specific instructions. Jesus then provided a few guidelines on how they should begin their mission. He told them that "repentance and remission of sins should be preached in [my] name among all nations, beginning at Jerusalem" (Luke 24:47). Also, "Ye shall receive power, after that the Holy Ghost is come upon you: and ye shall be witnesses unto me both in Jerusalem, and in all Judaea, and in Samaria, and unto the uttermost part of the earth" (Acts 1:8).

The apostles were to begin at Jerusalem and then move to Judea and Samaria. Not until they had covered these areas were they to move on to the more distant corners of the world. The apostles would not have been ready to take the Gospel into Gentile territory. First, they needed to do the necessary work closer to home. Not until they had gained experience were they ready to move on.

Today, the apostles' calling is still ours, but the way we carry out the command will look different from how the apostles did it. The Holy Spirit does speak through the brotherhood. Hence, it is the responsibility of a brotherhood to determine practical applications of Acts 1:8.

Let us analyze Acts 1:8 to see how this applies to us today.

1. "But ye shall receive power, after that the Holy Ghost is come upon you . . ." The Holy Ghost is an effective Guide and Counselor in the hearts of believers today. The Holy Spirit confirms Himself through the brotherhood, as well as convicting us personally whenever we err. He will never lead an individual to do something contrary to God's Word, nor will He reveal additional doctrines that are missing in God's Word. Seldom will the Holy Spirit lead us to do something contrary to the counsel of the rest of the brotherhood.

Even in a brotherhood that does not seem to be spiritually discerning, it is still wise to wait and not move ahead on our own. Other spirits also try to prompt us.[59] The

---

[59] 1 John 4:1.

Holy Spirit will prompt us in a still, small voice, and He will not lead us into confusion.

2. "And ye shall be witnesses unto me both in Jerusalem. . ." Jerusalem was home base for the apostles. They were to wait there until they received the outpouring of the Holy Spirit.

Jerusalem is a type of the church. Our foremost responsibility is to be witnesses to our brothers and sisters. The fundamental ingredient backing our witness is love. We will live in a way that our brothers can see that we are dedicated to Christ. When this trust and confidence exists, we will witness to each other by sharing our strengths, weaknesses, and insights. When we observe that one of our brothers has sin in his life, we will admonish him out of love.[60] Our leaders are responsible to preach the Word as they are led by the Holy Spirit. We are forgetful hearers and need to be reminded of Bible truths, though the sermons we hear cover no new concepts.

When we fail to be Christ's witnesses "in Jerusalem" we are not prepared to witness to outsiders.

3. "And in all Judaea . . ." Judea was the region around Jerusalem. It was the homeland of many Jews—Jews who knew and worshiped the God of the Old Testament but who still needed to believe in the Savior, Jesus Christ, as the only way to salvation.

Judea can be likened to professing Christians, who may say "Lord, Lord," claim the Holy Spirit, and share wonderful testimonies, but who lack obedience and true

---

[60] 2 Thessalonians 3:14–15.

discipleship. These professing Christians in "outlying Judea" will usually respect the lifestyle of those who abide in "Jerusalem." But they may tend to equate it with the culture of Jerusalem.

Our faithful witness in Jerusalem will not be hidden from those who dwell in Judea. Plenty of work remains in Jerusalem, especially in teaching the faith to oncoming generations. Yet the misconceptions of the dwellers of Judea need to be corrected. For too long, those of us in Jerusalem have determined that our witness there is the only witness needed to shine out to those in Judea. But these Judeans need to know how to add Scriptural obedience and discipleship to the profession of their faith. Therefore, the faithful witnesses at Jerusalem will at times need to leave their comfortable home base and reach out in presenting the truth to these nominal professing Judeans. If the inhabitants of Jerusalem are not willing to make some sacrifices, they are vulnerable to materialism and complacency.

Since these Judeans already profess to follow Christ, yet are not fully obeying Him, the challenge for Jerusalem is to know how to present the truth. Gentiles who have never heard of God will probably be more receptive to the Gospel, especially after they see the powerful effect of the Gospel in the lives of Christians. Nonetheless, we are Christ's witnesses both in Jerusalem and in Judea.

4. "And in Samaria . . ." The Samaritans were a mixed race with some Jewish blood. They worshiped God, but not according to the Mosaic Law. They had adopted some idolatrous practices. Thus, the Jews avoided the Samaritans

and refused to have dealings with them. But Jesus did not avoid witnessing to a Samaritan woman at Jacob's well, an action that surprised even His disciples.[61]

Samaria can be likened to people who know about God and who may confess Him as Lord, yet many of their actions are ungodly. Many modern Samaritans tend to deny the ultimate authority of God's Word by embracing some false doctrines that fit their thinking. Some may even declare that much of the Bible is no longer relevant. The citizens of Jerusalem must be discerning lest they become influenced by these idolatrous ways.

Here in America, the true citizens of Jerusalem are a minority. More and more souls are embracing the idolatry of Samaria. Given enough time, many Samaritans might even become atheistic. This could endanger the religious freedom of Jerusalem.

The kingdom of Jesus Christ recognizes the ultimate challenge to launch out into the deep so as to fish for the souls of these Samaritans. Today, many Samaritans, as well as many Judeans, are not open to the precepts of the kingdom. But at the same time, some Samaritans seem disillusioned by their upbringing and are seriously seeking for something better. However, they know little about the kingdom of God, and they don't know where to turn for help. While they might know something about Jerusalem, they tend to view it as an ethnic oddity, something to gawk at, not knowing it is a compelling answer. In another generation, Jerusalem may have more contact with seeking

---

[61] John 4:1–26.

Samaritans, but will we still have religious freedom when that time comes?

Our witness in Jerusalem should shine out to the Samaritans. Although we may have reasons for staying within comfortable Jerusalem, Jesus made it plain that His followers are to witness in Samaria as well as in Jerusalem. Do we perhaps fear that the Samaritans will "evangelize" the citizens of Jerusalem?

When Saul initiated a mass persecution against the early believers, their witness spread to the outlying regions of Judea and Samaria. But hadn't the believers' witness in Jerusalem already shone out to the Judeans, the Samaritans, and even to some of the Gentiles? Surely they knew where Jerusalem was located. But that was not God's method of evangelizing.

5. "And unto the uttermost part of the earth . . ." Are we willing to make further sacrifices? When we have committed ourselves to follow Jesus, are we willing to obey Him no matter where He leads us? To be Christ's witnesses to the uttermost part of the earth could mean never seeing our loved ones again. It might mean learning another language and adjusting to another culture in order to minister to the spiritual and physical needs of people who are vastly different from us. Nonetheless, they have eternal souls.

The Greek word translated *witnesses* in Acts 1:8 is *martus*, from which we derive our English word *martyr*. Throughout the centuries, many witnesses for Christ have been martyred. Is the cost too great? Jesus promised, "And every one that hath forsaken houses, or brethren, or sisters, or father, or mother, or wife, or children, or lands, for my name's sake, shall receive an hundredfold, and shall inherit everlasting life" (Matthew 19:29).

God Chooses His Witnesses

Since it is God's will that all men be saved, He wants His ambassadors to witness to those around them at every opportunity. It also means going into the highways and hedges, and even into foreign lands. Many countries contain countless unsaved people; they also need a witness. Of course, we realize that Christ does have witnesses now in other parts of the world.

Let us not make the mistake of thinking that we cannot be witnesses until we relocate to a foreign country. However, if God is clearly leading us to live among people of another language and culture, even thousands of miles away from home, are we willing to go? Or do the familiar comforts of our lifestyles, our occupations, and our communities hold us back? The same God who is with believers in an affluent nation like America is also with every believer in every part of the world.

Jesus did not promise that His commission would be easy to fulfill. And He did not promise that it would be easy to deny ourselves and follow Him. At times, we will meet situations in which we don't know what is best. But Jesus has promised, "I will not leave you comfortless: I will come to you" (John 14:18). The German rendering of this verse promises that Jesus will not leave us as orphans. He stated that all power belongs to Him in heaven and earth, and He will supply it to us as needed. Jesus also promised to be with us until the end of the world. And that promise remains in effect today.

Chapter Five

Honey for the Master

T he embers smoldered within the heap of rubble—the remains of what had once been a formidable structure. Nearly all of the unpublished Indian versions of the Bible, the newly cast type molds, the Bengali dictionary, and other equipment, had been reduced to ashes. As the three men surveyed the devastation, they said to each other, "Surely God will bring good out of this disaster."

What first appeared to be a terrible setback for William Carey and his partners turned out to be a hidden blessing. As news of the disaster spread across England, marvelous results developed. Many people who had been spiritually complacent were awakened and became burdened for lost souls. Thousands were moved to give sacrificially of their time and money. Out of this tragedy, new missionary zeal was born, causing the spread of the Gospel in India to advance in ways that would otherwise not have been possible.

The apostle Paul, likewise, saw good coming out of his unfortunate imprisonment. When the news reached his fellow Christians, they became bolder in witnessing. Thus, the Gospel spread in a way that Paul alone could not have accomplished. Moreover, even when some preached Christ out of faulty motives, Paul rejoiced that Christ was still being preached.

Ralph Palmer, a Mennonite man, traveled extensively over much of the United States, distributing tracts and installing Gospel signs. Sometimes handing out as many as ten thousand tracts in a day, Ralph distributed more than ten million tracts during his lifetime.

Although not everyone can be a Ralph Palmer, God can sow the precious seed through us. The results will be more outstanding than what Ralph Palmer managed to accomplish alone. After the building with its Bibles burned down, William Carey and his newfound partners accomplished more than they could have done otherwise. Together we can do more. The focus should not be on what one individual can accomplish, but on what God can accomplish through all of His children.

How Should We Fulfill Christ's Commission?

When Christ gave His last commission, He did not specify the methods that His people should use. There are no cookie-cutter answers for making disciples of all nations. People, cultures, and circumstances vary widely. What might work for one congregation might not work in another congregation attempting to reach out to a different culture.

First of all, we must be faithful witnesses in daily life. When every member in a brotherhood recognizes this, the door will open to corporate witnessing. When a brotherhood agrees to implement evangelistic strategies, it will bless those who need a witness as well as blessing brotherhood relationships.

In a spiritual brotherhood, different individuals may come up with different approaches to outreach. With a healthy brotherhood vision, individuals will lay down their preferred ideas and submit to what the church chooses.

For this reason, I am hesitant to suggest how we should evangelize, since every brotherhood will need to make its own decision. However, I can share a few ideas. In America, much of the population is literate. Sound Gospel literature can be a means of spreading the truth. Literature racks in public places can "witness" at all times. We can distribute catalogs that offer books and tracts for free, or at subsidized prices. Gospel signs along the road can sow truth. Nursing home services, prison ministries, and cottage meetings can be used if the opportunity arises. Our witnessing efforts may lead us to seeking persons whom we can invite to our worship services. Extended meetings could occasionally be held to test outsiders' interest.[62]

Keeping existing communities smaller and starting new

---

[62] By saying "extended meetings," I am referring to additional meetings held throughout the week, similar to Sunday morning services, and conducted by local or visiting ministry. I am not encouraging "revivalist-style meetings," where a dashing, fiery evangelist is hired to tickle the emotions of the people, and who does not respect the stand of the congregation that hired him. Even if extended meetings do not attract any outsiders, they are still beneficial.

communities in other regions is a method we should be using, instead of all crowding into one geographical region. Can we learn a lesson from the bees? When their colony grows large, these industrious little creatures will swarm and start a new colony elsewhere. This provides a stimulant for work and gives each creature the opportunity to gather much more honey than if they all crowded into one huge colony.

Like the bees, we too should be industrious in gathering much "honey" for the Master, who commanded His servants to "occupy till I come" (Luke 19:13). Our lifestyles, occupations, families, and evangelistic efforts should all contribute to extending His kingdom. Every region of the earth needs a faithful Christian witness.

Christ's last commission is not a job we can do alone. The Bible does not state that evangelization through outreach communities is the way witnessing must be done. Yet this method has been more successful than most other methods. The focus of apostolic evangelism was to establish churches in every nation over the world. In whichever regions people needed to hear the Gospel, the apostles planted churches.

When an outreach congregation is started, it becomes a home base for evangelistic activity in that area. The more our congregations spread out, the more souls we can effectively touch. Tract or book racks can be maintained in businesses within the new outreach community. We can minister to the elderly in nursing homes, hold cottage meetings, and start prison ministries close to the new outreach community. Witnessing efforts will always bear more fruit if coupled with our example and lifestyle. Moving into new regions will inevitably be more fruitful than occasionally traveling long distances to witness in those areas.

Migrating for the sake of spreading the Gospel can be financially difficult, especially for families that have growing children and an established financial base in their home community. Normally we tend to migrate to areas where land is more economical. But if we migrate for the purpose of establishing a Scriptural church, it might be difficult to find inexpensive land. Yet the people in other regions need to hear the Gospel too, and to see it demonstrated in our lifestyle.

Or we may wonder how we can provide for our households in a region where there are not many options for our traditional means of making a living. Jesus clearly taught us we are not to worry what we shall eat, drink, or wear. Our heavenly Father will supply whatever we need. Jesus' response to financial worries was, "Seek ye first the kingdom of God, and his righteousness; and all these things shall be added unto you" (Matthew 6:33).

Here is our answer. Seeking the kingdom of God will mean seeking what is best for others rather than seeking our own financial well-being. Certainly, we have reason to feel wary about relocating to urban settings, where the environment is not conducive to raising godly families or for maintaining a conservative lifestyle. Seeking God's kingdom will help us determine the most effective way to reach larger cities and suburban communities without exposing our families to the temptations there.

In essence, it is then the outreach congregation's duty to repeat the process of reproducing itself so that Christ's kingdom can continue growing. It is a never-ending cycle as long as our Lord tarries. We cannot do it alone. We must consider that every kingdom-focused church that dedicates its efforts to spreading the Gospel is a sharer of Christ's commission. We are all a part of this heavenly kingdom.[63] However, we can only do so much; therefore, we must pray to the Lord of harvest to send more laborers.

Should a Rural People Evangelize Urban Regions?

While we should evangelize as much as possible by keeping our communities smaller and continually starting new communities, this method is not possible or practical in some regions. Still, souls in these geographical locations need to hear the Gospel and to see it demonstrated by example.

Cities have posed a challenge to God's people throughout history.[64] Cain's descendants built the first cities; and after the Flood, Noah's descendants built the city and tower of Babel so they could all live in one geographical region. Lot's choice to move into an ungodly city cost him many heartaches when the city was destroyed and he lost his wife and sons-in-law. "For that righteous man dwelling among them, in seeing and hearing, vexed his righteous

---

[63] This is not saying that we should disregard fellowship boundaries. But it means that we will appreciate the evangelistic efforts of other denominations rather than looking down on them because of their weaknesses. See Philippians 1:18.

[64] This is not saying that true Christians cannot inhabit urban regions. We are not looking at what is possible, but what is ideal.

soul from day to day with their unlawful deeds" (2 Peter 2:8). Even though Lot remained faithful, he had to reap shameful consequences. Interestingly, in its early days, Christianity thrived mostly in urban centers.

For centuries, people living in urban areas were in the minority. In 2009, the urban population exceeded the rural population for the first time in history.[65] In the United States, 82 percent of the population is urban. Approximately 25 percent of the U.S. population lives in the metropolitan regions of Washington D.C., New York City, Los Angeles, Chicago, Miami/Fort Lauderdale, Philadelphia, Dallas/Fort Worth, Atlanta, Houston, Boston, and Detroit. These metropolitan areas have a population of four million or more. In addition, thirty-two other conurbations (extended urban areas) have a population exceeding one million.

Many of these heavily populated regions seem difficult, if not impossible, to evangelize. We have always shied away from traveling to these cities where crimes abound. Yet the souls in urban regions are just as valuable in God's eyes as souls in rural regions. What should we be doing to spread the Good News into regions not ideal for living in?

Many of us who embrace a vision for outreach pale at the thought of evangelizing in big cities. We are inclined to comfort ourselves with the fact that there is enough evangelistic work to keep us busy within rural regions and smaller cities. We don't want to neglect our evangelistic duties closer to home in favor of distant mission work.

Nevertheless, our evangelistic duties do include people

---

[65] Jason Mandryk, *Operation World,* pp.1 and 861, 7th edition.

in metropolitan regions. Imagine approaching Jesus in person and asking Him, "Jesus, when you said that we should be your witnesses to the uttermost part of the earth, did you also mean the massive metropolitan regions?" What would Jesus' answer be to us? Wouldn't He promise to be with us wherever He leads us?

So now let's look at another method for evangelizing. Consider with me a system of itinerant outreach, the concept of traveling to regions where people need to hear the Gospel. Our Lord appointed His twelve and later seventy disciples to do itinerant outreach. He did not send them alone, but by twos. The early Anabaptists also sent itinerant evangelists in groups of two and three throughout the German-speaking regions of Europe. During the evangelists' absence, the church provided for the needs of their wives and children. Many of these evangelists never returned, paying the ultimate sacrifice for their work. Yet in this way, the Gospel spread to other regions.

Itinerant outreach could take place today in the form of a congregation appointing two or more mature brethren to travel to large cities to witness. The details of such a mission would need to be decided by the church. The congregation should look after the needs of the families of the brethren they send out.

We need to find ways of reaching urban areas without surrendering to the harmful influences. Our witnessing efforts should focus on discipling sincere seekers to understand Biblical values and develop healthy lifestyles, such as living closer to the land. This has been a strength of our people, and it has the potential to transform the lives of seekers. We ought to explore ways in which we can both reach out to cities and promote a conservative lifestyle. Another idea is to do a mass mailing of literature in an urban area, with the sponsoring church's contact information on the literature.

Thus far we have considered several approaches to outreach. No doubt other ideas merit consideration. One thing to remember is that if the church at home is not being cared for, more outreach is not better. Each congregation needs to decide what it can handle without neglecting its own needs.

Opportunities and open doors will vary. No individual, church, or organization can do everything, but everyone can do something. In the end, the faithfulness of a Christian will not be judged by how extensively he evangelized, but by his daily obedience to *all* of Christ's commands.

Progress Is Evident, But Much Potential Exists

We rejoice at the progress in world evangelism. Even in restricted and hostile nations where Christians are persecuted for their faith, thousands of unbelievers are being converted to the faith. God's kingdom is increasing daily. But Satan still has many souls in bondage. Masses of humanity have never heard the name of Jesus. Who will go?

In this harvest, the global needs exceed the workers. One individual cannot make all the difference in a lost and dying world, nor can the united efforts of one congregation. Jesus said, "The harvest truly is great, but the labourers are few: pray ye therefore the Lord of the harvest, that he would send forth labourers into his harvest" (Luke 10:2). Many more workers—indeed, all Christians—are needed. With the collective efforts of all true Christians, it would only be a matter of time until every person on earth could hear the Good News!

When I was in school, the teacher gave us a math problem. A farrier offered a customer a deal for shoeing his horse. He charged one penny for the first nail, two pennies for the second nail, and doubled the cost of every nail up to thirty-two nails—eight nails on each of the horse's four hoofs. What was the total cost for shoeing the horse?

The answer is astounding. If the customer could ever come up with the money, the farrier would never again have to work. He would be a millionaire forty-two times over, and all that from charging only a penny for the first nail. By doubling and redoubling the cost, the figure escalates amazingly fast.

Now let's apply this mathematical concept to the work of evangelism. We know that more than one dedicated kingdom-focused Christian inhabits this earth. However, let us suppose that in this year, 2017, there would only be one dedicated person who is part of Christ's kingdom. Through his evangelistic witness, this Christian would win one soul to the faith. Now there would be two Christians. Next year, in 2018, these two Christians would each win one soul to the faith, and there would be four Christians. If this would go on, every Christian winning one soul every year, how long would it take until the whole world would be converted to Christianity? If the Lord tarries, by 2050, the whole world would be converted! That's right; this revival would take only thirty-three years.

Of course, this concept is unrealistic in a world where Satan is feverishly working to hinder the spread of God's kingdom. For the millions of souls truly converted to a saving faith in Jesus Christ, millions of other souls are falling away from the faith they once professed. Millions more continue to be blinded by the gods of this world.

I trust you can see, though, that our labors can bear more fruit than we might imagine. We can make a difference in the eternal destiny of a few souls. And if those souls embrace the same vision and zeal for the kingdom, they too will be counted as laborers in the harvest field. The ripple effect will keep on increasing.

Any endeavor that focuses on Christ's kingdom and decreases potential for materialism is a move in the right direction. As a brotherhood, we might not always accept or endorse all methods of outreach. Yet our overall vision must be to actively reach out to those who are lost. A brotherhood should not minimize the need for outreach by focusing solely on self-preservation. Preservation of time-tested traditions and values does play a part in maintaining a stable, Biblically conservative brotherhood. However, preservation and evangelistic outreach must be kept in balance so that one is not emphasized above the other. Both must be properly maintained.

The Missing Spoke

Chapter Six

Good Tidings—and We Hold Our Peace

T he blazing sun was beginning to disappear into the western horizon, signaling the end of another day. Four leprous men hovered near the city entrance. Foremost on their minds was the grim reality that, unless they found food soon, they must surrender themselves to certain death.

Samaria had been besieged by the Syrians and, as a result, was experiencing a terrible famine. From inside the city gates came the pitiful cries of children, malnourished and weak. If only God would perform a miracle and send food! Finally one leper spoke up. "If we could enter Samaria, we would die because of the famine. But if we sit outside the city, we will also die. Why don't we visit the Syrian camp? Perhaps they will take pity on us and give us something to eat. The worst we can expect is that they will kill us. We have no choice but to resign ourselves to death."

Putting their plan into action, the four lepers arose in the gathering twilight and headed toward the Syrian camp, where they expected to receive no mercy. Imagine their surprise to discover that not a single person was in the camp. Everyone had fled, leaving behind an abundance of food, clothing, treasures, horses, and donkeys. With delight, the lepers ate and drank until they were filled. They entered a second tent and carried out silver, gold, and other treasures.

Surveying their accumulation of treasures, which they planned to hide, they stopped abruptly. "This is not good," they said to each other. "This is a day of good tidings, and we hold our peace." Rushing back to Samaria, they broke the news of their discovery.

The king of Samaria found the news incredible. "Suppose the Syrians are waiting somewhere in the field to take us captive, so they can seize our city," he reasoned. Finally the king sent messengers to the Syrian camp, who returned with clothing and vessels of value. Thus, the king thus knew it was safe, and the people went out and looted the camp. The famine was finally broken.[66]

Wouldn't it have been tempting for the lepers to hoard all the food and treasures for themselves? Instead, they discovered the joy of sharing. Today, we possess a treasure incredibly more valuable than the food and treasures discovered in the Syrian camp: we have the treasure of the Gospel, salvation, and a faithful heritage. Suddenly it dawns

---

[66] 2 Kings 7.;Ibid, pg. 861-862

on us, "This is a day of good tidings—and we hold our peace."

When we have found such a valuable possession, are we willing, like the lepers, to share with those who need it? If we have discovered something essential to building the kingdom of Christ, wouldn't we want others to know about it too?

We recognize that in times of spiritual famine, when Bibles are forbidden or not readily available, people are more receptive to accepting the discovered treasure. Here in America, the situation is different. There is a famine here as well, but it is a dearth of desire. The treasures of the kingdom are readily available, but many Americans simply won't accept them. Many are spiritually destitute and don't even recognize it. Hence, they tend to reject our offer of these treasures.

When we have discovered something precious, we want to make sure we don't lose it. Many churches have set out to share these kingdom treasures but end up losing them in exchange for the treasures the world has to offer.

Many plain groups have jealously guarded these treasures. But why are we so reluctant to share? This is a day of good tidings, yet we hold our peace. Do we fear we will lose our treasures? The lepers could easily have convinced themselves that if they shared with all the inhabitants of the city, there might not be enough left for them. Yet they found that there was plenty for everyone. There are enough pearls for everyone on earth.

In short, our plain churches have found many reasons to hold their peace. Let us analyze some of them.

Why Do We Hold Our Peace?

One reason is our fear that outsiders will misunderstand our message. We feel more confident that they will not misunderstand our faith if we simply show them our consistent example. More is caught than taught, we reason. If we began teaching them, we could be setting ourselves up for losing respect if they saw that we are not consistently living what we are teaching.

Some of us have concluded that mission work is not good because we should live our faith and not talk about it. But if we talk about our faith, does that imply that we are not living it? According to the Bible, part of living our faith is to "be ready always to give an answer to every man that asketh [us] a reason of the hope that is in [us] with meekness and fear" (1 Peter 3:15). We are to talk about our faith when someone approaches us with questions. Should we not also take the initiative to approach those who are in the kingdom of the world?

Others hesitate to evangelize because it might offend someone. We do not want to force our faith down someone's throat; but if we are trying not to offend anyone, aren't we trying to do what Jesus did not? Because of the truth Jesus proclaimed, He offended many people, especially the scribes and the Pharisees. Jesus said, "Blessed is he, whosoever shall not be offended in me" (Matthew 11:6). There is no way around it—people will be offended. Certainly we do not want to offend anyone deliberately; but we must recognize that no matter how careful we are, the message will sometimes offend people.

We know that many outsiders respect our way of life. Some have probably been inspired by our example and committed themselves to follow Christ more fully. Some may have been offended because of a plain person's inconsistencies. Our example, whether good or bad, is a witness to everyone we meet.

But do outsiders know why we live the way we do? Do they see us following a different lifestyle because of our loyalty to a heavenly kingdom? Or do they think our lifestyle is only a cultural oddity? In the rare situation that an outsider decides to join a plain church, is it because he desires to genuinely walk in obedience to God? Or is he attracted only to certain aspects of our culture?

Sometimes we think that society is just not open to the truth; otherwise, people would be looking for Scriptural churches to join. If they were truly seeking, they could find out where our churches are located. And if they were truly serious, they would even be willing to learn the German language. Most of these people own at least one Bible or New Testament. If they would simply put into practice what they read in their Bibles and would look to Christians who are examples in living the faith, society would soon be on the right track again.

Living our faith is vital. Many outsiders are indeed correct that living a restricted lifestyle does not earn one's salvation. Hence they see no need to affiliate with the Plain People.

What if outsiders mistakenly surmise that we hold to kingdom practices—such as nonconformity, marriage as a lifelong commitment, nonresistance, restricted communion, feet washing, the Christian woman's head covering, brotherhood assistance instead of insurance, and separation of church and state—because those practices are part of an Anabaptist culture? This misunderstanding should be corrected. We believe that these teachings which set the Plain People apart are not merely old-fashioned, peculiar "Anabaptist doctrines." We observe them because they are true Bible doctrines.

In this area, our lifestyle cannot be totally effective if we are unwilling to testify about it. We do not do well to hold our peace. We must also evangelize by whatever methods are Scriptural and church-honoring. We need to somehow present the truth to those who have false concepts of the Gospel, though many will not accept the truth.

We believe that God expects more from us as Plain People than He does from those who were not taught as we were. We also understand that the punishment will be more severe for those who knew better and still ignored God's law than for those who never were enlightened. Does this mean we should not promote the truth, because God will then be merciful to those who never had a chance? What if we could be doing something but do not do it? Will God hold us accountable for holding our peace? "Therefore to him that knoweth to do good, and doeth it not, to him it is sin" (James 4:17).

We must remember that many people view us as a subculture, although they might be aware of an underlying religious foundation. People can never see the complete picture of the kingdom of Jesus Christ merely by observing us from the outside, just as we cannot see the complete picture of someone's family life merely by looking in the windows of their home.

It is our duty, as citizens of Christ's kingdom, to tactfully present the truth. Our lifestyle and example alone can never completely do this. We should explain that we are more than just another culture.

If we as a church do not have any evangelistic strategy in place other than our lifestyle and example, we become especially vulnerable to Satan's lure of materialism. Reaching outside our circles in a Scriptural manner can strengthen the church and boost the spiritual vitality of its members.

Would We Lose Our Nonresistant Values?

Another reason some hold their peace seems to be based on nonresistance. Some think it is wrong for the "quiet in the land," who refuse to be involved in politics or to hold any position in government, to go about actively talking about their faith. They think that if they go out and offer their faith to others, they are resisting evil works and are no longer nonresistant.

So then, does this mean that Jesus, the apostles, and the early Christians were not nonresistant? Did Jesus and His followers refuse to speak up because they feared the people's response?

John the Baptist warned King Herod that it was not right for him to have his brother's wife. This "slip of the tongue" cost John his freedom and eventually his life.

When Paul preached to the people in Ephesus, the whole city grew into an uproar. Some cried one thing, and some another.[67] Should Paul and his companions have preached in a place where the people would have been more receptive to their message? Should they have ignored the Diana worshipers? That would have been easier.

Jesus tenderly pleaded with the people, but He also stated what they must do to follow Him. He never forced anyone to follow Him, but He did speak against the evils of His day. This is why many of the Jews hated Him.

Jesus viewed every individual as a potential heir of His kingdom. Therefore, He taught us to be nonresistant and not to hate our enemies, each of whom could become a citizen of heaven. Instead, we view them as souls who can be changed through the power of Christ. If we murder an enemy, his chance to repent is gone.

In any evangelizing endeavor, we will at times face resistance. But Spirit-filled Christians will not resist evil men even when sinners resist the Holy Spirit. If a person shows no interest, we should not keep pressuring him.

Would We Lose Our Humility?

A pearl that Old Order churches esteem is humility. After the Anabaptists migrated to America, they exchanged suffering for humility. To live on the frontier with only the necessities fostered humility. But when the Industrial Revolution set in, goods formerly considered luxuries became affordable. Gradually the conservative Anabaptist groups adapted to a more affluent culture. In the meantime,

---

[67] Acts 19:32.

revivalist influences were increasing. Conservative leaders sounded the alarm, yet this affluent lifestyle was already too firmly rooted. To continue identifying with humility meant to preserve the old ways of worship.

Sometime in history, the precious pearl of humility was trodden underfoot when the emphasis in some churches shifted to outreach. For this reason, we tend to feel that if we evangelized more, our humility would be endangered.

We all know the opposite of humility. Pride takes no effort because it comes from our carnal nature. And pride is subtle. If we think we do not have it, we do. Humility is exactly the opposite. If we think we have it, we have lost it. The danger of taking pride in being plain and traditional is as great as the danger of worldly pride.

Pride has been the downfall of many individuals and churches in their evangelizing efforts. Yet if we abstain from evangelizing, we are not free from pride. Pride can snare us in many ways. Only through God's grace can we be humble.

What if our plain churches agreed to drop our distinctive dress standards because we feared some member would take pride in his plain clothes? What if we decided that plain clothes attracted needless attention? What if we decided to drop our separated lifestyle because we take too much pride in it? Wouldn't some non-Plain People be surprised?

Some individuals do take pride in their plain dress and separated lifestyle. But we would never think of dropping these earmarks of our faith. Is this reasoning any different from avoiding outreach because of its association with pride?

Avoiding outreach does not constitute humility. We must evangelize from the same motives we have for practicing the other tenets of our faith. The Man who evangelized most effectively was also the most humble Man. The same pride that can enter into evangelizing can also enter into every other aspect of our lives. Everyone is vulnerable to pride.

What grounds, then, do we have for emphasizing humility? If we emphasize humility, it has eluded us. Humility is the fruit of an individual who has fully yielded his life to Jesus' control. Plain clothes and simple living do not make a humble Christian, yet a humble Christian wears plain clothes and lives simply.

When we compare our lives with Christ's, we realize that without His grace we are nothing. Only then can we obtain humility. And then we will faithfully do whatever He bids. We must say, "We are unprofitable servants: we have done that which was our duty to do" (Luke 17:10).

Can we testify that we have always done our duty? Truly, we are unprofitable servants. We have no reason to take pride in our accomplishments. Were it not for God's grace and mercy, we could never find our way to heaven, no matter how many good deeds we did.

Since we are not perfect, we will make mistakes at times in our outreach endeavors. We must look at these failures as learning experiences that can foster humility in us.

The founders of the Old Order movement identified pride as the motivating force in the "great awakening," the Mennonite revival in the 1800s. For a humble people, this meant avoiding symbols of pride. In the attempt to correct the errors of others, we may have overreacted and embraced the opposite of the errors around us—but have come no closer to Scriptural revival. True revival demands self-denial, full obedience to the Bible, and a return to God's purpose for the New Testament church: to be a light and a salt to the world and to evangelize in the humility and simplicity of the Gospel.

Must We Evangelize to Be Saved?

What is man's role and God's role in soul-winning? For too long we have felt more comfortable in thinking that if God wants souls to be saved, He will cause it to happen in His own way and timing. When we hesitate to evangelize, it may be because we do not want to take matters into our own hands. Instead, we choose to leave the salvation of souls in God's hands, since His Spirit can convict. We must not underestimate God's power to change lives. He could choose to convict souls through a personal encounter. He could speak in an audible voice or through some dramatic experience. But God often chooses not to use these methods. How humbling to realize that God usually uses imperfect men as instruments in His hands! He wants to use us to accomplish His will. Will we cooperate and allow Him to do His amazing work?

It is not God's will that one soul should be lost. Mankind was created in God's image, and every soul is of equal value in God's eyes. When we accept God's gift of salvation, He pours His Spirit into us. He wants to give us the same compassion for lost souls that He has. We want to help the lost in whatever way God desires. We are instruments in His hands.

As Christ's servants, we have a duty to evangelize—a duty we fulfill because we want to. Evangelizing is a manifestation of Christ's love in our hearts. It is our obligation, but not our salvation.

Maintaining Purity in Worship Services: Are Seekers a Threat?

Many plain groups have been taught to worship in a formal manner. To maintain this formality, we expect everyone from the children to the grandparents to be attired uniformly. This eliminates fashions and represents oneness in our gathering. We consider the church to be one big family. To maintain these "family" ties, we expect everyone to comply with the "family" standards, just as we like everyone in a home to comply with the standards of the household.

This raises a question as soon as seekers step in. When someone wants to worship with us but does not dress like we do, we tend to see him as a threat to the uniform image of our assembly.

Inviting others into our services raises more questions: Do we want a group of seekers who are not dressed according to our standards worshiping with us on a regular basis? Worse yet, what if they are indecently clothed? We value the assembly place as a haven from worldly influences. We yearn to protect our children from indecent exposure. For these reasons, should we invite outsiders to worship with us?

This problem, like the German language, has no easy

solution. The best question to ask ourselves is, "What would Jesus do?" We should consider the nature of the church. Whose kingdom are we building? Is it Christ's kingdom or our own Amish or Mennonite kingdom? God is no respecter of persons. If God shows no partiality, why should we?

The apostle James expressed this idea clearly: "My brethren, have not the faith of our Lord Jesus Christ, the Lord of glory, with respect of persons. For if there come unto your assembly a man with a gold ring, in goodly apparel, and there come in also a poor man in vile raiment; and ye have respect to him that weareth the gay clothing, and say unto him, Sit thou here in a good place; and say to the poor, Stand thou there, or sit here under my footstool: are ye not then partial? . . . But if ye have respect to persons, ye commit sin, and are convinced of the law as transgressors" (James 2:1–4, 9).

In God's sight we are equal whether we are plain or not, and whether we speak German, English, or any other language. In light of the passage above, shouldn't it make us uncomfortable to realize we could be showing partiality to our own brethren and not giving seekers the welcome they deserve? This Scripture passage is relevant at all times. Its message cannot be misunderstood. Partiality is sin, no matter what other Scriptural concepts we use to justify partiality.

How can we maintain purity in our worship services and still accommodate seekers? The problem is, we would prefer to see seekers immediately comply with our dress code and submit themselves to the rest of our standards so that none of our weaker members are negatively affected. Yet these expectations are not realistic. Seekers need time to sort out their priorities, and they will want to attend our worship assemblies for a while before they become a part of us. We do not do them or ourselves a favor by pressuring them to make quick decisions.

We have reason for concern if immodestly dressed people want to worship regularly with us. On the other hand, if they show genuine interest, they probably already know to dress modestly, even if not in conformity with our church's dress code. Also, seekers may feel out of place when they are dressed differently, and they may desire to fit in sooner. It is not wrong to request that they dress modestly, but it is wrong to be partial against those who are different.

We have touched some extremely sensitive subjects. You may be thinking, *I can follow the logic, but it is different from what we have been taught.* True, these concepts may be different from our tradition. But are they contrary to the Scriptures? If the Scriptures support these concepts, can we refuse them? Do we value our traditions more highly than the principles in God's Word?

I fear that the root of the matter may be our natural biases. Instead of molding ourselves around the Scriptures, are we not molding God's Word to fit our traditions?

Chapter Seven

Christ's Last Commission— Apostolic Only?

A s Matthew reflected over the past forty days with his resurrected Lord, he thought of how good life had been and how he hoped it would continue this way indefinitely. Little did he realize that today would be the end of an era; after today he would not have the opportunity to see the Master. Nor did he realize that he would later face the choice between denying his Lord or losing his life. After an eventful three years of following the world's greatest Teacher, Matthew's disappointment of seeing Him arrested, crucified, and buried in a tomb was almost more than he could bear. That is, until three days later, when he greatly rejoiced to be able to walk and talk with this Teacher again.

Jesus had told His eleven disciples to meet Him on Mount Olivet. Matthew anticipated another session of learning at the feet of his Master. Again he marveled that, out of all the thousands of other Jews, he had been chosen by this great Teacher to witness His marvelous power.

As Matthew and the other ten disciples gathered on the mountain, they wondered what their Master would say that day. When Jesus appeared, they worshiped Him, even though some of them doubted. Jesus' reassuring words and presence were what they needed. After some brief, simple instructions, Jesus led His eleven disciples to Bethany, where He lifted up His hands and blessed them. Then, without warning, His feet were swept off the ground. Awed, the disciples gazed heavenward at their departing Master until He disappeared into the clouds. So intent were they on catching one more glimpse of their Teacher, that they did not notice the two men in white robes. Suddenly one of the white-robed figures spoke. "Ye men of Galilee, why stand ye gazing up into heaven? this same Jesus, which is taken up from you into heaven, shall so come in like manner as ye have seen him go into heaven" (Acts 1:11).

Matthew later recorded in his Gospel the last words Jesus had spoken, His last commission to His followers: "Teach all nations" (Matthew 28:19). Mark recorded the same message with a different wording: "Go ye into all the world, and preach the gospel to every creature. He that believeth and is baptized shall be saved; but he that believeth not shall be damned. And these signs shall follow them that believe; In my name shall they cast out devils; they shall speak with new tongues; they shall take up serpents; and if they drink any deadly thing, it shall not hurt them; and they shall lay hands on the sick, and they shall recover" (Mark 16:15–18).

The message of these passages is clear. They explain that the Gospel is intended for people of all nations, languages, and cultures.

Christ's last commission included a special application for the apostles. The word *apostle* literally means "a messenger sent out." These men had a unique obligation during this transitional period as the New Covenant was revealed. Since they were eyewitnesses to the life and calling of Jesus,[68] He appointed them to this special ministry.[69] This included the power to perform miracles, the authority to institute Christ's church under the New Covenant, and divine inspiration to write epistles which today are included in the New Testament canon.

Analyzing Christ's Last Commission

It is comfortable for us to think that Christ's last commission was indeed an exclusive mandate for the apostles. But this comfort can result from poor reasoning.

I believe that the apostles' calling differed from the calling of the Christian church afterward. One conservative writer observed the fallacy of every Christian being expected to fulfill Christ's last commission in the same way. He wrote about how a stirring message on the commission was delivered to a captivated congregation. After the message, one man commented to his wife that if everyone would take the message seriously, the parking lot would be

---

[68] John 15:27; Acts 1:21; 2 Peter 1:16.
[69] Luke 5:3–16; Matthew 10:1–4.

completely empty the following Sunday, since everyone would be on the mission field.[70] It seems obvious that God does not ask everyone to move away from their homes at the same time.

Although opinions differ, the command to "teach all nations" clearly means that the church's obligation extends farther than its own people. Every Christian is a missionary. Every congregation is a "mission congregation." A mission field exists just as much at its own door as on the other side of the world.

This raises questions. Do we fully recognize our duties? Is our lifestyle and example fulfilling this commission? We do not want to overlook the fact that "mission work" is God's role. It's not that He is limited, needing man's help. But He has chosen imperfect mortals to be His ambassadors.[71] We are instruments in God's hands. Are we willing to be used as He wants to use us?

Let us consider some aspects of Christ's last commission, as Matthew records it.

1. "All power is given unto me in heaven and in earth." Christ holds the ultimate authority on earth. We cannot build on any foundation other than Him. Through His Spirit dwelling within us, He enables us to live victoriously in Him and gives us strength and courage to do things we wouldn't be able to do on our own. Because of Christ, every knee must bow and every tongue must confess Him as Lord. No other power exceeds His.

Jesus recognized that His last commission would be no

---

[70] Samuel Martin, "Misguided Mennonite Missions," 6.
[71] 2 Corinthians 5:20.

easy task. But He promised the apostles and all Christians down through the ages to assist them in fulfilling all of His commandments. Through Christ's power within us, all things are possible. This includes overcoming challenging obstacles such as racial and cultural barriers. The more we realize we can do nothing good of ourselves, the more God's grace can abound in our lives.

If this commission was intended only for the apostles, then the Holy Spirit's power likewise was only for them, and not for us.

2. "Go ye therefore, and teach all nations, baptizing them in the name of the Father, and of the Son, and of the Holy Ghost." Did Jesus commission His disciples to teach and baptize only if the nations flocked to them? Of course not. He said, "Go ye." By what authority can we say that the teaching and baptizing part of this commission is still for the church today, but not the going part? "Go ye." What else can it mean? *Go* has the completely opposite meaning of *come* or *stay*, yet it seems we have confused the terms.

Someone once explained how ordained leaders fulfill Jesus' command to go. They show up when we gather for worship. They do not stay at home, waiting to fulfill their calling until someone comes to them. Therefore, this command to go is being fulfilled.

But is it being fulfilled in its entirety? Does it cancel the church's obligation to go to all nations and to every creature? I think not. Jesus' command to go and His mention of all nations and every creature is clear.

If Christ's last commission applied solely to the

apostles, the ordinance of baptism also applied only to them. In that case, no ordained leader should baptize repentant believers upon their confession of faith. How can these two commands—to baptize and to preach to all nations—be separated? Opinions vary as to how this should apply, but it clearly means that the church also has a duty to preach the Gospel to those outside her immediate fold.

3. "Teaching them to observe all things whatsoever I have commanded you." Some denominations place much emphasis on going, preaching, and baptizing, and then their actions indicate that they believe they have fulfilled Christ's commission. Yet the hardest part of this commission is to teach all nations to observe what Christ has commanded. The only possible way to effectively teach "all nations" the "all things" of Christ is to practice them ourselves. In our various plain churches, Satan has failed in convincing us to discard some of the "all things" Christ commanded. But it seems Satan has succeeded in convincing us that if we practice the rest of the "all things," we can ignore the first clause of Christ's commission.

4. "And, lo, I am with you alway, even unto the end of the world." Jesus closed His last commission with a promise. Can the promise be separated from the rest of His commission? Can we claim this part if we say the rest is only apostolic? If Jesus meant "even unto the end of the world" only for His apostles, He must have expected His apostles to live until the end of the world.

Jesus' promise "even unto the end of the world" is not to be taken as an apostolic application meaning, "unto the ends of the earth." In Greek, the word *aiōn* (Strong's #165) is translated by the Luther German and the King James translators as *world*, means "age." This Greek word is derived from the root *aei* (Strong's #104), meaning "continued duration." Strong's #166 gives another derivative, *aiōnios*, which means "perpetual." It is translated as *eternal* or *everlasting*. It is no mistake—Jesus meant He would be not only with His apostles in helping them fulfill this commission, but also with every Christian until the end of the world. The promise is connected with the commission.

Then What about Mark 16:17–18?

In his gospel, Matthew chose not to mention the signs. Mark, on the other hand, seems to imply that the commission applies as long as the signs last. Is this a contradiction?

We find it most comfortable just to dismiss this whole passage—to assume that the promise of signs, and hence Christ's whole commission, was only intended for the apostles. Is this passage truly saying that? To whom did Jesus promise these signs? Only to the apostles? No. He unmistakably promised that "these signs shall follow them that believe." Since these signs aren't literally following us, does that make us unbelievers?

I think not. We are misunderstanding something. Is Jesus' kingdom a literal kingdom or a spiritual kingdom? Is He the physical Head or the spiritual Head of the church? The Bible teaches that Jesus' kingdom is spiritual; He is the spiritual Head of the Church. Thus, it is possible that the signs Jesus promised are also primarily spiritual, rather than physical.[72]

Usually when God chooses to withhold something from us, is it not because He has something better in mind? "Verily, verily, I say unto you, He that believeth on me, the works that I do shall he do also; and greater works than these shall he do; because I go unto my Father" (John 14:12).

Jesus promised all true believers[73] that they would do "greater works" after He returned to His Father. This is possible because Jesus has sent His Comforter, the Holy Spirit, to dwell within the hearts of men. The indwelling presence of the Holy Spirit makes Christ's followers spiritual. Hence, Jesus may have meant that these "greater works" are spiritual in nature.

Consider further the account of Pentecost. Then, the evidence of the Holy Spirit was accompanied with visible tongues of fire. If we no longer see this demonstration, does that imply that the indwelling presence of the Holy Spirit was solely intended for the apostles? Is the Holy Spirit no longer an effective Counselor today in the life of a Christian if there are no visible tongues of fire? The Holy Spirit can work in the hearts of men without physically revealing Himself. Likewise, it is reasonable to maintain that the last commission of Christ is still in force, even if it is no longer accompanied with visible signs, miracles, and wonders.

Miracles did have a place in the transitional period

---

[72] Miracles and signs still occur today, but often in cultures that do not have access to the written Word. It is not something for us to seek after, but God sometimes chooses to reveal Himself in certain situations much like He did in the early church.

[73] Notice the words, "He that believeth on me." Jesus was not speaking merely about His apostles.

before the New Testament canon was complete. They reminded the people of the divine nature of Christ and served to usher in the spiritual kingdom. But spirituality and salvation have never been measured by miracles.

For this reason, we should not feel that faith is lacking since we cannot perform miracles. But when we apply verses 17 and 18 figuratively, things start making sense. These signs Jesus promised represent the saving power of the Gospel. "Casting out devils" refers to taking control of wrong thought patterns and praying to God to rebuke any demons trying to control us and others. New speech will be the outward evidence of an inner transformation of the heart.[74] The serpents and deadly poisons represent false doctrines. Laying hands on the sick represents the renouncing of sin in our own lives and being instrumental in helping sinners to be spiritually healed.[75]

We cannot necessarily heal those with physical sickness. We cannot usually speak in tongues like the apostles did at Pentecost. We cannot even of ourselves cast out devils. Neither can we handle deadly serpents or drink deadly poisons without suffering consequences.

But we can, through prayer and fasting, take action so that His Spirit can effectively move, and sick souls can be spiritually healed. We can speak with new tongues, our speech reflecting spiritual interests rather than carnal interests. By God's grace we can confront false doctrines,

---

[74] Matthew 12:34.

[75] This is the writer's interpretation and is not meant as the final authority. God can still cause supernatural wonders to occur whenever He chooses.

A reviewer notes: "What parent hasn't laid his hands on a sick child and prayed for the child? We don't make a big deal out of it, but it happens."

which have the potential to bring spiritual death. Aren't these the "greater works" in John 14:12 that Jesus promised to all believers? In this sense, then, Christ's last commission is still binding in our age.

Christ's Ultimate Authority

Perhaps some of us feel more comfortable in believing that the only evangelistic efforts described in the New Testament are those of Christ and the apostles. Their authorization to evangelize was authenticated by supernatural miracles, signs, and wonders. But the precedent they set for the congregations afterward was different. Does the fact that the apostles did not emphasize Christ's last commission in their epistles give evidence that this commission was especially directed to them and not to the church in general?

Why do we need further evidence from the apostles' records? Jesus Christ is the final authority for us, as He was for them. None of His commands have been contradicted by the apostles. Jesus Himself stated, "All power is given unto me in heaven and in earth."

Indeed, the call to reach out is not isolated to the last several verses in Matthew 28 and Mark 16. The wedding parable in Matthew 22 and the great supper in Luke 14 portray the urgency of going out and inviting souls into the heavenly kingdom. One of the verses even charges us to compel them to come in. The word *compel*, in this case, does not mean to manipulate anyone. Rather, it means to plead and persuade with urgency.

Some ordained leaders and others will sometimes quote

Romans 10:18 to prove their view that Christ's last commission was indeed, only apostolic. But they fail to consider the context of the rest of the chapter. Read verse 16: "But they have not all obeyed the gospel. For Esaias saith, Lord, who hath believed our report?"

Romans 10 was originally written about the Jews who rejected Christ. The beginning of the chapter reveals the apostle Paul's intense desire that his own people, the physical Jews, would be saved. Then in verses 14–15, he writes about those who do not believe in Christ: "How then shall they call on him in whom they have not believed? and how shall they believe in him of whom they have not heard? and how shall they hear without a preacher? And how shall they preach, except they be sent?" In verse 17, Paul goes on to say, "So then faith cometh by hearing, and hearing by the word of God." The Luther German translation of this verse shows that faith comes through preaching, and preaching by the Word of God.

Paul wrote that the sound of the Gospel went over the whole earth — past tense (verse 18). Earlier, he explained why it is still necessary to preach the Gospel. According to verse 16, not all have believed the report. Also, the question of how someone can believe in Him if he has not heard (written in future tense) proves that if the Gospel does not continue to be preached in an area where it was rejected, only a generation later some people again may never hear.

A valid question is then asked: How can someone preach unless he is sent? Far too often, individuals have appointed themselves to preach the Gospel. This action is hardly

Scriptural. Would part of the blame lie on the church for failing to appoint preachers?

The definition of *preach* in verse 15 does not refer to the example of our lifestyle. If it did, this verse could be paraphrased to say, "And how shall they preach through their consistent, godly example except they be sent?" No, this is not consistent with other Scriptures. All of us already are called to leave good examples.

Likewise, Colossians 1:23 would be saying that nothing more is left to do. We must take verse 23 in the context of the rest of the chapter. Even though the Gospel had in a sense come to the whole world, the apostle Paul recognized his duty to continue preaching, as evidenced in verses 27–29: "To whom God would make known what is the riches of the glory of this mystery among the Gentiles; which is Christ in you, the hope of glory: whom we preach, warning every man, and teaching every man in all wisdom; that we may present every man perfect in Christ Jesus: whereunto I also labour, striving according to his working, which worketh in me mightily." If Christ's last commission was already fulfilled (verse 23), then the apostle Paul was out of his calling. And verse 28, written in present tense, was not for Paul's day or ours.

The Example of New Testament Christians

Early Christian believers reached out with the Gospel to those outside their own circles. After Stephen was martyred, Saul began a mass persecution against the church at Jerusalem. As a result, many Christians fled to other regions. Acts 8:4 says, "Therefore they that were scattered abroad went every where preaching the word." We read more in the eleventh chapter of Acts about this dispersal. After Peter's encounter with Cornelius, and his defense to the Jewish Christians at Jerusalem who criticized his actions, Acts 11:19 shifts back to the Jewish Christians who had been scattered abroad. "Now they which were scattered abroad upon the persecution that arose about Stephen travelled as far as Phenice, and Cyprus, and Antioch, preaching the word to none but unto the Jews only."

If this "preaching the word" only meant leaving an example, or answering the questions of non-Christian Jews who approached them, how could the Christians have "preached" only to the Jews? Both Gentiles and Jews lived in these areas. Paraphrasing the last part of verse 19 to mean "preaching the word through their consistent, godly example to none but unto the Jews only" would imply that these believers were not a consistent, godly example to the Gentiles. Obviously, that doesn't make sense.

Consider also verse 20, which says that some of the Christians were men of Cyprus and Cyrene. These men, after receiving the Gospel preached by the Christian Jews, in turn preached the Gospel to the Grecians at Antioch. As a result, there were now also some Gentile believers.[76]

---

[76] The meaning of the word *Grecians* in Acts 11:20 is debatable. Were these Antioch Grecians Gentiles, or were they Hellenistic (Greek-speaking) Jews? Reference sources do not agree. Even the *Zondervan's Pictorial Bible Dictionary* contradicts itself by referring to them as Gentiles in one place (see "Antioch," pages 47–48) and as Hellenistic Jews in another place (see "Grecians," page 324). However, *Strong's Concordance* authoritatively defines these Grecians as Hellenistic Jews.

Interestingly, the Luther German implies that these men from Cyprus and Cyrene preached to the Grecians, in addition to the Jews. Would the Bible make a distinction if these Grecians had been Jews? The German says: "*...die kamen gehen Antiochien und redeten auch zu den Griechen und predigten das Evangelium vom Herrn Jesus.*" (Literal translation: They came toward Antioch and spoke also to the Greeks (Grecians) and

When this news reached the church at Jerusalem, they sent Barnabas to Antioch to provide assistance. This is the first New Testament record of a Gentile congregation being established. It did not happen because of the apostles traveling to Antioch to preach the Gospel. God was working through faithful believers, not merely through the apostles, to spread His message.

If it is correct that Christ's last commission was intended only for the apostles, then these Jewish believers obviously exceeded their calling. However, we read of no hint that the apostles told the Jewish believers that what they were doing was solely an apostolic mandate.

Acts 11 does not state the methods these Jewish believers used to propagate the Gospel. Did they take the initiative? Did they boldly proclaim the Gospel to every Jew within hearing distance? Was it more personal, such as friend to friend? Or did they wait until one of the non-Christian Jews inquired about their newly found faith? The New Testament does not say.

Why Didn't Paul Endorse the Apostles-Only Concept in Philippians 1?

This brings us to another aspect of Christ's last commission. The apostle Paul wrote the following words while he was in prison:

---

preached the Gospel of (the) Lord Jesus.)

Moreover, this passage is in context with the Gentiles' entry into the New Covenant (possibly happening immediately after the conversion of Cornelius and his household). The congregation at Antioch has been considered by historians as the first congregation consisting of mostly Gentile Christians, because Antioch was where the Judaizers from Judea determined to yoke Christianity to Judaism. (See Acts 15.)

At any rate, the men of Cyprus and Cyrene preached the Gospel; the Gentiles eventually felt the impact.

> But I would ye should understand, brethren,
> that the things which happened unto me have
> fallen out rather unto the furtherance of the
> gospel; so that my bonds in Christ are manifest
> in all the palace, and in all other places; and
> many of the brethren in the Lord, waxing
> confident by my bonds, are much more bold to
> speak the word without fear. Some indeed
> preach Christ even of envy and strife; and some
> also of good will: the one preach Christ of
> contention, not sincerely, supposing to add
> affliction to my bonds: but the other of love,
> knowing that I am set for the defence of the
> gospel. What then? notwithstanding, every
> way, whether in pretence, or in truth, Christ is
> preached; and I therein do rejoice, yea, and will
> rejoice. Philippians 1:12–18

Although he was an apostle, he was not miraculously
released from prison so he could continue his preaching.
Paul said that some indeed preach Christ out of wrong
motives. Here would have been the apostle's prime
opportunity to explain that Christ intended evangelistic
work only for the apostles. If this was correct, why didn't
Paul explain this concept in Philippians 1?

Paul was not endorsing the actions of those who
preached Christ out of contention. What he meant was that
the Gospel was still being spread, even though some people
had wrong motives.[77] In other words, God can make good

---

[77] It would perhaps be tempting to conclude that Paul was referring to their example and
actions. Nevertheless, something does not quite add up. How can actions of envy and strife

come forth, despite evil intentions or wrong motives.

Likewise, we should rejoice that many souls all around the world are finding Christ today, even if the methods of many missionaries seem questionable. We supposedly trace our ancestry to the barbarous Teutonic tribes of northern Europe, who first heard the Gospel from Roman Catholic missionaries. If God caused good things to come out of unscriptural groups and methods of furthering His kingdom, He can bless any church that seeks to obey Him.

Ambassadors in Christ's Stead

"Now then we are ambassadors for Christ, as though God did beseech you by us: we pray you in Christ's stead, be ye reconciled to God" (2 Corinthians 5:20). Few Christians would apply this verse only to the apostles. Can this ambassadorship be fulfilled merely through our lifestyle and example? Second Corinthians 5:17–20 reveals that being an ambassador does not merely mean setting an example. According to verses 17 and 18, Christians are new creatures in Christ. As part of the covenant, God has also entrusted to us the ministry of reconciliation.

Would Jesus have fulfilled His charge of ambassadorship had He decided to allow His lifestyle and example to be the only influence in our reconciliation? Now we are ambassadors in Christ's stead. We have a ministry of reconciliation patterned after the example of Christ.

We cannot duplicate Christ's life and mission. But we can

---

testify of Christ? Impossible! If Paul was rejoicing that some good was coming forth, even through those who preached Christ out of wrong motives, by what authority can we criticize those who out of good will, would advocate a broader scale of outreach?

make applications that fulfill the requirements of this ambassadorship. The church has a responsibility to determine applications so that Christ's last commission can be fulfilled.

Some may agree that Christ's last commission was meant for the church of all ages, but not in the same way as for the apostles. Since the church is required to make applications today, its leaders might suggest that the mere presence of a Scriptural church in the midst of a degenerate society is a sufficient application.

Would such an application achieve the intent of the commission? Are we biased enough against evangelism to ignore a lack of obedience to Christ's commands?

The Missing Spoke

Chapter Eight

The Widening Gulf

D uring the 1700s the Anabaptists did not face the death penalty, but they were still a despised people. They were often forced to pay heavy toleration taxes, and they never knew when the bubble of toleration would burst.

In 1763, Catherine the Great, ruler of Russia, extended an invitation to various groups of Germans to settle millions of acres of land that the Turks had vacated. Since this tsarina was a native German, she recognized the Germans, especially the Anabaptists, as being industrious farmers.

At first the Anabaptists did not accept the offer. In 1786, Catherine the Great sent a native German representative named George von Trappe to the Anabaptists in Prussia. By this time, political and economic conditions had changed, and the Mennonites showed more interest.

The empress promised them sizable tracts of free land. She offered a startup loan, free transportation to Russia, religious freedom, and the privilege to govern their own colonies. She allowed them to organize their own churches and schools, to keep their own language, and to have unconditional exemption from military service. There was one stipulation, however. They were not allowed to evangelize or make converts from the Russian state churches.

To the oppressed Anabaptists in Prussia, this offer sounded too good to pass up. To verify the offer, the Mennonites in Prussia sent two men, Jacob Höppner and Johann Bartsch, to visit Russia and report back to them.[78] In the next several years, more than two hundred families emigrated to Russia, with more to come later.

Whenever a major migration is attempted, it takes time to settle in. Cornelius J. Dyck, a historian with Russian roots, wrote of the hardships the first Mennonites in Russia faced.

> Pioneering difficulties were so many in these early years that most of the immigrants became quite dissatisfied. Disease and death took a heavy toll. Rains made the mud huts even muddier. Horses were stolen or lost for lack of fences. Wood for construction was slow in arriving and of inferior quality. The promised government assistance of 500 rubles per family was delayed, much of it arriving eight years later. The people were very poor; even elder Bernhard Penner had to wear homemade sandals to church instead of shoes. There were unsettling clashes with marauding tribes.

---

[78] Horsch, *Mennonites,* 271; Daniel R. Lehman, *The Russian Mennonites,* 42–46.

Nevertheless, by the turn of the century the 400 families had become established in fifteen villages and were farming approximately 89,100 acres of land.[79]

In spite of their rough start, prosperity kissed them during the next several generations. Their prosperity made the native Russians jealous. The Mennonite farmers who hired Russian peasants to work for them did not treat them kindly, and paid them poor wages. This caused resentment from the Russians against the Mennonites.

In spite of a mass exodus to America during the 1870s, their numbers continued to increase. By World War I they numbered about one hundred thousand.[80]

Dark clouds were brewing on the horizon. Rumors of wars became a reality. The Bolshevik Revolution broke out. Lawless soldiers roamed the land, attacking people and looting and destroying property. The Mennonites witnessed their possessions disappearing in a short time.

Then a spiritual tragedy happened—a tragedy we hope will not be repeated. A number of young Mennonite men initiated a *Selbstschutz* (self-defense plan) to defend themselves and their colonies. This provoked animosity from the Russians. For many years the Mennonites had professed to be nonresistant; but when their lives and property were threatened, they defended themselves.

However, a majority still believed it was wrong to defend themselves. They were embarrassed about the self-defense

[79] Dyck, *Introduction,* 172.
[80] Horsch, *Mennonites,* 273; Lehman, *Russian,* 138, 150, 166.

movement some of their people had started. But even though they were not at fault, nonresistant Mennonites still faced the same animosity as the members of the Selbstschutz. In colonies where there was no self-defense movement, Mennonites did not suffer as much.[81]

What lessons can we glean from this? If history should repeat itself, how would we respond? If God should send the fires of tribulation or persecution into our midst, the hay and stubble will be destroyed; but the gold will become purer. Could God someday test our works?[82]

Dealing with the Root

We have no choice as to when God will allow history to repeat itself by causing our period of peace and prosperity to end. However, we can choose how to respond. Let's look at several factors that had a bearing on the apostasy of the Russian Mennonites.

First, they were not being persecuted for their faith. They were considered reputable workers and respectable citizens. Instead of being hated, they were being praised. It is no wonder that Jesus expressed this concern: "Woe unto you, when all men shall speak well of you!"(Luke 6:26)

Secondly, material prosperity was within their reach. Because they were industrious workers, they accumulated wealth. They did not have to worry that the government would confiscate their goods or force them to pay heavy taxes. They lived in a land with religious freedom, and God blessed them materially.

[81] Horsch, *Mennonites*, 285–287.
[82] 1 Corinthians 3:12–16.

Thirdly, the new generations that came along experienced nothing other than the peace and prosperity of Russia.

Last but not least, these Mennonites lost their evangelistic zeal. Forbidden to engage in such activity, they became an exclusive, cultural entity. The lack of outreach did not directly cause their decline, but it did cause stagnation. Is it not probable that this stagnation, coupled with prosperity, caused their apostasy?

It seems that when the Russian Mennonites agreed not to evangelize, they lost a spoke in the wheel of their faith. Could it be that this loss weakened the other spokes?

The history of the Russian Mennonites is lamentable because they failed to pass on the faith. They continued their forms of worship and embraced a visible piety. They appeared to be serving Christ, but in reality they had lost their vision.

They passed on a lifestyle to the next generations without passing on the faith. One unfavorable aspect of the Russian Mennonite colonies was that their leaders tended to use political power to enforce compliance. This came about because their colonies were not completely under the authority of the Russian government. The Mennonites were required to comply with some laws, but the Russian government expected them to be a self-governing subculture. This provision blurred their view of the separation of church and state.[83]

The factors causing the downfall of the Russian

---

[83] Lehman, *Russian,* 50–51, 63–65, 72–73; Horsch, *Mennonites,* 273, 275–276; Bender and Smith, *Their Heritage,* 69.

Mennonites are prevalent in North America today. The only difference is that the plain churches in North America have not yet been tested like the Mennonites in Russia were.

Satan uses various tactics to persuade Christians to compromise their faith. Today in North America, Satan is using God's blessing of material prosperity as a weapon to undermine our faith. If God should send physical persecution or tribulation, what would prevent those who are not firmly grounded from losing their faith?

The early founders of Anabaptism had a vision of a Scriptural, voluntary believers' church. This vision fed an active evangelistic witness. But before the Mennonites emigrated to Russia, they had lost this vision of a pure New Testament church. As a result, the Russian Mennonites were willing to eliminate evangelism.

How Are We Vulnerable Today?

Today our various plain churches recognize Christ's last commission as non-optional in two of its three components, namely, to teach and to baptize. The first component, "to go," means "to take initiatives beyond the comfortable boundaries of Jerusalem." We have largely ignored this facet of Christ's commission. Despite this, Christ's last commission is being fulfilled. The Gospel continues to be preached. Souls continue to turn from darkness to light. The church continues to flourish and grow, its presence illuminating the dark corners of the world. God's Spirit is still at work, convicting many souls.

Yet a gulf has appeared. Since today's church cannot duplicate the apostolic application of Christ's last commission, it needs to determine its own applications accordingly. As a result, some plain groups have concluded, "The apostles' mission was to travel around the world, preach the Gospel, and establish Christian churches all over the world. Our mission today is to be a light to the world and a salt to the earth. This can best be done by being a distinct, peculiar people, living a separated lifestyle, being a consistent example, raising our families in the fear of the Lord, and earning our bread by the sweat of our brows."

Is this the church's sole mission today? Is this application sufficient? These questions deserve careful thought. We who have been raised in a plain setting often are not thankful enough for our upbringing, and for being spared the problems prevalent among those of other backgrounds. Church leaders have expressed concern that if we start evangelizing, the values we cherish will suffer. Let's analyze the basis for this concern and seek to find a balance.

It's easy to see what a "missing spoke" did for the Waldenses and later for the Russian Mennonites. Are we in the midst of a spiritual tragedy as well? What has penetrated many plain churches, resulting in the missing spoke of Biblical outreach?

Remember the requirements Jesus gave to those who wished to be His disciples? Jesus required some radical changes in their lives, to test where their loyalties lay. For many followers of Christ, it is possible and honorable to have an occupation and raise a family for the sake of His kingdom. Nevertheless, have we perhaps become vulnerable? By passively witnessing through our example, have we become overly comfortable within the boundaries of a lifestyle that appears acceptable? Do we feel that we do not need to make tremendous sacrifices or exert extensive efforts to proclaim the Gospel to unbelievers and nominal Christians? Hence, we face the danger of becoming entangled in materialism. Our faith is in jeopardy. That is what happened to the Russian Mennonites. Let's learn from history!

What Do We Choose?

God created man both a physical and a spiritual being. He gave man the choice to fill the void within. Would man choose to fill it according to the desires of his body or according to the desires of his spirit?

What do we choose today? We can choose to fill our void with money, fame, sports, social life, entertainment, eating, hunting, pleasure trips, immorality, tobacco, alcoholic drinks, or music. Or we can choose to focus on farming, raising families, building businesses, or doing evangelistic work. But if we form an excessive devotion to these good things, are they any less dangerous than some things on the first list? How many of the things mentioned above are morally wrong in themselves?

Our devotion must be to Jesus Christ and His kingdom. How do we become devoted? We adopt His mindset and revolve everything we do around Him. We love Him and obey His teachings. We love the Lord with all our heart, soul, mind, and strength—and we love our neighbors as ourselves.[84] We seek the good of others, doing to them as we

---

[84] Matthew 22:37–39; Mark 12:30–31; Luke 10:27.

want others to do to us.[85]

If we are more concerned about making a living, having a good work ethic, living a separated lifestyle, or raising a family than we are about the kingdom of Christ, we stand in danger. If we excessively devote ourselves to evangelism, wandering here and there while neglecting our duties at home, we also stand in danger.

Once we devote ourselves to Jesus Christ and His kingdom, God will show us how to live as whole people, in which our physical lives are integrated with our spiritual lives. Our work, hobbies, vision, outreach—every part of what we do—will be pursued with the mentality that we are doing it for Christ. We will be willing to do what He says and go where He leads us. We will do all for His glory, since we rightly belong to Him. Our lifestyle will reflect a desire to be used by God in whatever capacity He chooses.

Put this to the acid test. Living right is important. Raising families is also. A good work ethic and a separated lifestyle cannot be minimized. But if the church overemphasizes these values in a way that puts Christ's kingdom secondary, we lose our focus. When we find it hard to identify with Christ's kingdom of sacrificial love, we stand on dangerous footing. Something else is becoming our first love, no matter how good and right it may be.

The life and example of our Savior consisted of service to others. His life was a life of sacrificial love.

What Did Christ Truly Teach?

As we prayerfully consider Christ's teachings, we do not

---

[85] Matthew 7:12; Luke 6:31.

see that Christ considered work, family, and a structured lifestyle as the most significant matters. As was discussed in Chapter 1, His primary purpose for coming to earth was to establish His kingdom. Whenever He called someone to follow Him, He required that person to sacrifice material interests. Jesus made the terms and conditions plain. A true follower must sometimes choose between Christ and family ties.[86]

We find it hard to believe that Jesus meant for all of His followers to forsake their families and everything they own. His teaching on this principle must not be misunderstood. If a Christian needs to make a choice between following Christ or remaining loyal to his family, there should be no question which he should do. Following Christ needs to be foremost, even if a Christian faces opposition from those he loves. On the other hand, if our family and friends are also seeking to follow Christ, we are hardly being fair to them by appointing ourselves to a mission and not considering their feelings.

Jesus laid out an object lesson. He asked, "Who is my mother? and who are my brethren? And he stretched forth his hand toward his disciples, and said, Behold my mother and my brethren! For whosoever shall do the will of my Father which is in heaven, the same is my brother, and

---

[86] One reviewer warned that this statement could be misunderstood. He commented, "I had a friend who was involved in prison ministry (accepted, but not supported by the church). After a number of years with no converts, he lost his family to the world or to more-liberal churches, all in the view of following Christ."

The author of this book comments, "If God has given us a family, He expects us to give them our first priority. (See 1 Timothy 5:8.) Raising a family should not be the ultimate in the lives of Christians who are married, but it is an integral means of furthering Christ's kingdom. Those who have a family should search for ways of reaching out that do not tear the family apart."

sister, and mother" (Matthew 12:48–50).

Jesus taught against materialism. "But as the days of Noe were, so shall also the coming of the Son of man be. For as in the days that were before the flood they were eating and drinking, marrying and giving in marriage, until the day that Noe entered into the ark, and knew not until the flood came, and took them all away; so shall also the coming of the Son of man be" (Matthew 24:37–39).[87] "Likewise also as it was in the days of Lot; they did eat, they drank, they bought, they sold, they planted, they builded; but the same day that Lot went out of Sodom it rained fire and brimstone from heaven, and destroyed them all" (Luke 17:28–29).

Surely God would not punish people for eating, drinking, marrying, buying, selling, planting, and building! These activities are not wrong in themselves, but they become wrong when they divert our focus from Christ's kingdom. Satan uses legitimate activities to ensnare mankind.

The prophet Ezekiel tells why God took drastic measures with Sodom and Gomorrah. "Behold, this was the iniquity of thy sister Sodom, pride, fulness of bread, and abundance of idleness . . . neither did she strengthen the hand of the poor and needy. And they were haughty, and committed abomination before me" (Ezekiel 16:49–50).

Jesus promised His followers, "Verily I say unto you, There is no man that hath left house, or parents, or brethren, or wife, or children, for the kingdom of God's sake, who shall not receive manifold more in this present time, and in

---

[87] See also Luke 17:26–27.

the world to come life everlasting" (Luke 18:29–30). Jesus forbade one man to bury his father.[88] Jesus detected that this man had reservations about becoming one of His followers.[89]

Also, the apostles' writings tell us how to live. These writings were inspired by the Holy Spirit and include precepts that Jesus did not teach during His earthly ministry. The Epistles reinforce working hard, making a living, raising a family, leading congregations, and submitting to a body of believers. We understand that Jesus valued these precepts.

If there is no Gospel, there can be no Epistles. If we believe that a theology based on the foundation of Christ would forbid us to evangelize, we have tricked ourselves.

Where do we find the basis for our traditional values? Are we not making Christ's Gospel secondary to the apostles' teachings if we minimize His commission because we fear we would neglect our families and lose some precious values if we focused on reaching the lost?

Is Evangelistic Outreach the Cure?

In a previous section, we discussed the danger of focusing on making a living. If the primary focus should not be on our way of life, should it be on evangelistic outreach? Unless our focus centers on the kingdom of Jesus Christ, all of these good aspects of living are in vain. Lifestyle is not the hub of this kingdom. Neither is evangelistic outreach. The

---

[88] Luke 9:59–60.
[89] Perhaps this man's father was still living, and he would rather have waited to follow Jesus until after his father was dead and buried.

hub is the kingdom of Jesus Christ. Evangelistic outreach is merely one of the spokes in the wheel. Other spokes in this wheel include strong families, faithful church administration, submission to the church, personal commitment and devotion to God, application of Bible principles, consistency in example, obedience to Christ's teachings, a separated lifestyle, and a strong work ethic. When one of these spokes is broken, the wheel is weakened.

Should we repair the broken spoke of evangelistic outreach? Definitely. But is that enough? Will the wheel be strong again? Not unless we strengthen the rest of the spokes.

Let's consider a few ways evangelistic outreach could be a blessing to the church. One aspect of evangelistic outreach is migrating to another location to plant a Scriptural church and Gospel witness. If we knew that the church might someday ask us to sell our farms or businesses and move to an outreach location, wouldn't that provide an incentive for us to live more simply now? There would also be less comparing among ourselves, since all the brothers and sisters should realize they are eligible for such a calling. It should remind us that we are only strangers and pilgrims on the earth. The possibility of a call to relocate could affect our perspective on making a living. We would also want to help with church-assisted outreach work in our present communities, which might mean taking time off from our busy schedules. We would hold our financial well-being more loosely.

With a vision for outreach, we recognize the importance

of examining our whole walk of life. The faithful church with an evangelistic vision will continually strive to obey Christ's teachings and to make consistent applications to Biblical principles, including a separated lifestyle and a strong work ethic.

For this to happen, we must redirect our focus. We are citizens of another country. We are ambassadors for Christ's kingdom. Our primary focus must be on ways to extend His kingdom. We must live separate from the world around us, find honest ways of making a living, and raise our families with love so that future generations will be a part of Christ's church. "But if any provide not for his own, and specially for those of his own house, he hath denied the faith, and is worse than an infidel" (1 Timothy 5:8).

Yet our daily living must somehow be kept in proper perspective. Christ's purpose for His church on earth is to be a light and a salt to those who are not yet part of His kingdom. We must direct our first love completely to God. That includes seeking His will for reaching out to lost souls around us. Where we have been complacent, we must repent. Then we must do what it takes, even if others misunderstand us.

Will family life suffer if we focus more on evangelizing? This indeed can happen. But it does not need to be that way if we are discerning. We need united direction from the brotherhood to find a balance in evangelizing without neglecting our families.

Chapter Nine

Separation and Outreach—Are They Compatible?

S hortly before the Israelites were ready to enter Canaan, God spoke through Moses and forbade anyone to move his neighbor's landmark. These landmarks defined the boundaries marked out for each tribe. Deuteronomy 27:17 pronounced a curse on the man who moved a landmark. The wise man Solomon wrote, "Remove not the ancient landmark, which thy fathers have set" (Proverbs 22:28).

Today we have the teachings of Jesus Christ to guide us on the narrow pathway. The applications of Christ's teachings can be likened to landmarks defining where the boundary line runs between the church and the world.

Various Scriptural church groups have set landmarks in various places. The way our forefathers set landmarks does not necessarily mean their conclusion is the only right way.

Unless we use God's wisdom to set landmarks that more fully reinforce the underlying principles of the Christian faith, it will seldom work to move a landmark to a place that better suits our preference.

Satan entices us to move these established landmarks bit by bit, convincing us it doesn't matter. Everyone around us is doing it too. Time will reveal whether their relocation is a good idea or not. It is tempting to think that some landmarks are no longer applicable in our time. However, our sons and daughters may lose their way if they can no longer locate the landmarks.

Our forefathers were not perfect. We would like to assume they always set landmarks according to Scriptural principles, but that would be a biased conclusion. The founders of the Old Order movement possessed insights on where the church might end up. Regretfully, many of the descendants of the progressive movement have dropped almost all vestiges of their heritage, and they can no longer be recognized as a separate and peculiar people. But the conservative sector set landmarks that more fully embraced the way of humility, self-denial, and separation.

Negative aspects of the liberal wing caused a reaction, which worked against some changes for the health, growth, and stability of the church. Thus our ancestors set a few landmarks hastily. Two of these landmarks are the non-promotion of evangelistic outreach and the misuse of the German language.

By reacting to these two landmarks, some have carelessly moved or discarded other landmarks. They have failed to appreciate and maintain the ones set according to Scriptural principles. Generations later, their descendants no longer appreciate the valuable landmarks.

Today we might question whether we can evangelize and still maintain the remainder of these landmarks. We have reason to be concerned. Many congregations who encourage a greater level of outreach have compromised some landmarks. Seekers coming into their congregations found it difficult to embrace some landmarks that we regard as priceless. As a result, landmarks have been adjusted or discarded. The pressure to become more like the world to win the world is tempting.

Many plain churches have placed barriers around themselves in order to remain a separate people. We as Plain People are used to our ways of doing things, and those from other backgrounds are used to their ways, making it almost impossible to reconcile the differences. Does that mean we may throw up our hands, admit defeat, and ignore our duties in reaching out?

History proves it never has worked for the church to adopt the culture around her. To remain separate from the world, the true church forms a subculture that expresses separation while existing within the culture of the world. In the first chapter, we read that Jesus Christ came to establish His kingdom. It is a separate kingdom existing within the physical boundaries of political kingdoms. Christ's kingdom portrays a separate focus and a different culture from the world's kingdoms. That is the only way Christ's kingdom will survive. Our greatest concern is whether we can maintain our separation *from* the world while reaching out to those *in* the world.

We recognize, however, that the kingdom of Jesus Christ is not restricted to our denomination or culture. When we promote Jesus' kingdom, we are not implying that everyone must join our denomination to enter the kingdom. If we value our lifestyle and culture, we will want to maintain it. But the Gospel we must preach is the Gospel of the kingdom and not necessarily the applications we have made to our lifestyle.

Changes—Growth or Drift?

Many plain churches are wary of changes. We prefer to be grounded in the stable, time-tested traditions of the past. It is good to evaluate where potential changes might take us and then to discern whether that represents growth or drift in the church.

A congregation refusing to acknowledge some change will become stagnant, and a congregation endorsing rapid changes will end up drifting. But a congregation that recognizes Christ as its Head will see some change as beneficial if it more closely identifies with and exalts Christ's kingdom.

Deliberate evangelistic outreach can appear daunting to churches that have traditionally resisted change. Many of us fear outreach because we are too shortsighted to gauge whether these efforts will bless our churches or backfire. Yet Jesus has authorized His church to take the Gospel to all nations.

When a brotherhood of believers has a vision for

reaching outside their comfort zone, Christ will bless them and protect them from inherent tendencies to be assimilated into the world. Christ is able to help His church maintain a pure vision in the same way He is able to keep His children from falling. Both of these promises are ours.[90]

Thus, it takes an active faith to depend on God to save His children and His church from the attacks of the enemy. If we could visibly view the mysteries of God and foresee the future, we would no longer need faith. Faith is believing that which is impossible to see with our natural sight. Could it be a lack of faith if we fear that evangelistic efforts will end in assimilation?

For successful outreach, we must not think that becoming more like the world will win the world. If our lifestyle and culture has been a blessing for those of us who have been brought up that way, why wouldn't it also be a blessing for others who are truly seeking something better?

Modern Technology—an Indispensable Evangelistic Tool?

As a people who have traditionally rejected automobile ownership, we may be tempted to change this tradition in light of a desire to evangelize. We may reason that if we had our own automobiles, we could move about more freely and reach more people. Not owning automobiles can be a disadvantage for us in some ways. Yet the more I think about it, the advantages of not owning a vehicle still outweigh the disadvantages.

A brother from a church that allows automobiles once discussed with me the pros and cons of the automobile in

---

[90] Matthew 16:18; Jude 24;

outreach. I asked him, "If we had ready access to the automobile, wouldn't we tend to bypass our evangelistic responsibility closer to home by traveling to distant cities to be a witness?" He agreed that this indeed can happen.

The reasons for making limited use of the automobile in outreach are just as strong as the reasons for our non-automobile lifestyle in general. Certainly, with our slower means of transportation, we spend more time on the road to travel shorter distances. In the long run, however, we probably spend less time on the road than the typical American. We tend to make our trips more worthwhile. Our efforts do not have to be impaired by our limited use of automobiles.

Or think of how many more people we could reach if we evangelized with radio, television, and the Internet. But we reject these forms of communication because we recognize the dangers of these devices. We would never think of offering someone a drink of pure water in a cup used to measure out poisons, would we?

Certainly, different churches draw their lines differently in the use of technology in lifestyle and evangelism. The churches successfully monitoring the use of modern technology while remaining Biblical and conservative deserve commendation. But if our church has traditionally rejected certain technology because of its associated dangers, we are not gaining anything by suddenly accepting these same things under the guise of using them as evangelistic tools. Tacking the word *evangelistic* to something does not make it less dangerous. Many Christians in the past, with devotion to the kingdom, have effectively evangelized without modern technology. We can do the same, and God will bless it in the same way He has blessed us all along.

Back to Acts

History tells of churches that compromised so that seekers would find it easier to adapt. Generations later, it has become evident that the world these churches were trying to evangelize has instead influenced the churches. Our plain churches are not immune to this danger.

There are no easy answers. How rigidly should a church cling to every last aspect of its culture? Which parts of our culture should we never compromise? When would an alternative be acceptable so that seekers navigating their way into our churches would not feel overwhelmed?

I do not have answers to all of these questions. But if we go back to the Book of Acts, we can glean insights on how the New Testament church at Jerusalem handled this type of situation.

Here, we see another separated people, the Jews, who believed they were God's favored people. This belief did not change easily. Even Christ's apostles believed it. For Peter, it took a vision from God to verify that the Gentiles could be fellow heirs of the Gospel.[91]

Like our Old Order churches, the Jews had their dialects they spoke with each other. They still used Hebrew in their worship services. The Law of Moses, along with other traditions handed down through the years, was important

---

[91] Acts 10.

to them. Now, the Jewish Christians were trying to observe Jesus' teachings as well. All these years, the Jews had considered the Gentiles unclean, not as people special to God. But they were finding out that God viewed the Gentiles on an equal basis with them.

The situation came to a crucial point when certain Jewish Christians required the Gentile converts at Antioch to become Jewish proselytes and observe the Law of Moses before they could be saved.[92] The controversy was becoming heated, so they agreed to meet with the apostles and elders at Jerusalem.

After the disputing at the meeting died down, Peter got up and spoke of his experience: how God had chosen the Gentiles to become equal heirs of the Gospel, and how He had poured out His Spirit upon them in the same manner as He had on the Jews on the day of Pentecost.[93] Peter wondered how they could expect the Gentiles to convert to the Law of Moses, when neither the Jews themselves nor their forefathers had been able to keep it fully?

Then the apostle James concluded that the Gentiles should not be required to follow the Law of Moses. But he expressed his concern that they should abstain from four practices. Otherwise, they were free to follow Christ's teachings.

What world would we live in today if Jewish Christians had succeeded in converting the Gentiles to Judaism? Would not the spread of Christianity have been obstructed? We have no way of knowing how many Jewish Christians

[92] Acts 15.
[93] Acts 10:45.

returned to nominal Judaism during that time, but we do know that the true church of Christ eventually consisted of people from all backgrounds, including Jews, Romans, Greeks, and people from uncivilized and barbarian cultures. Every group making up the church of Christ was unique.

We have no foundation in the New Testament to believe that the one true church of Christ scattered over the known world was confined to an exclusive culture, or *Ordnung,* beyond the Gospel of Christ. Passages like Romans 14 and 1 Corinthians 8 indicate that there were differences among Christian believers of various backgrounds. These differences were acceptable as long as they did not oppose or contradict the Gospel. Further, the Jewish Christians were now allowed to do some things they formerly had not been allowed to do. And the Gentile Christians had a sensitive conscience against meat that had been sacrificed to idols, even though the meat in itself was not defiled. The apostle Paul taught them that Christian liberty is not liberty if it is a stumbling block to those who are weaker. For this reason, Paul concluded that he would not eat meat if it caused his brother to stumble.

Are We in Error to Cling to Tradition?

How does the advice that the apostle Paul gave the Jewish Christians on how to relate to the Gentile Christians apply to us today? How can we reconcile differences between backgrounds and cultures so that prospective converts will not struggle to adapt? Are we in error to cling to a traditional lifestyle, language, and culture? Are we binding an excessively heavy burden on seekers who would like to join our churches?

First, we need to consider that part of the mission of the New Testament church is to evangelize, not necessarily to make converts a part of our church. Evangelizing does include teaching the necessity for uniting with a Scriptural church. Once a seeker is ready to find a church, we should help him find one rather than pressuring him into joining our own church. Our duty only goes as far as inviting souls into Christ's kingdom. But we do want to make a seeker feel welcome if he attends our services.

Second, are we not clinging to the same errors of the Jewish Christians if we view our traditions, lifestyle, and cultural practices as attaining our salvation? Although our lifestyle does not earn our salvation, it is not wrong to require converts to make certain changes to fit in better. If a person can make changes to conform to the world, why should the church be apologetic to require conforming to its standards, which are based on the Bible?

Even though the Gentile Christians were not bound to the Law of Moses (and neither were the Jews), the apostles laid down four requirements for the Gentile Christians. "For it seemed good to the Holy Ghost, and to us, to lay upon you no greater burden than these necessary things; that ye abstain from meats offered to idols, and from blood, and from things strangled, and from fornication: from which if ye keep yourselves, ye shall do well. Fare ye well" (Acts 15:28–29). I understand this passage to mean that the church, as a congregation or conferring body, does carry a responsibility to apply standards and to require converts to make these necessary changes if they want to have membership. Tolerating a double standard within the brotherhood will weaken unity and invite confusion and discord.

Third, we must evaluate our traditions in light of God's Word. When a practical application upholds an underlying Scriptural principle, such as separation, we should be slow to discard the application. Any traditions and practices that do not seem connected with the Scripture should be re-evaluated lest we burden potential seekers with unnecessary things.

Of course, this is not as easy as it sounds. How did it go for Gentile converts joining Christian churches of Jewish background? Did the Jewish Christians still cling to some Mosaic traditions if they expressed a practical application of Scriptural principles? Did they require Gentile converts to learn the Hebrew and Aramaic languages? We weren't there, so we don't know. But it seems hard to imagine, especially on language.

But we do know that it would not have worked for the apostles and the early Christian church to evangelize had they interpreted outreach within the frame of reference of the Jewish culture. Hence, we must be slow to gauge the sincerity of seekers merely by their willingness or reluctance to conform to our Bible-based standards and culture. And we never want to interpret outreach success according to how many converts we can win to our church. Our duty is to evangelize so that the wicked may be warned. We need to leave the outcome of their destiny to God. It is not in our place to judge those who respect our convictions and yet see no need to unite with a Biblical church. Eternity alone will reveal the results of the good seed sown through evangelistic efforts, though we might not see much fruit now.

We need to discern which aspects of our culture could be changed without compromising separation, and which aspects we can never change. This is not easy; not everyone will agree which changes to make. We need to implore God for wisdom.

Chapter Ten

"And How Shall They Hear?" The Dilemma of the German Language

Levi and the Snow Church — an Allegory

A s Levi reflected over the past three years, he grew despondent. He had tried so hard, but now he felt like a failure. He was no closer to mastering that difficult Japanese dialect than when he had first determined to learn it.

Levi would have felt differently had there been no other way to communicate with these "snow church" people other than learning Japanese. The problem was, Japanese was not the only language these people could fluently speak. Situated in a remote region in northern Quebec, these people were used to communicating with outsiders in French. Levi had learned French with difficulty after moving to Quebec, and his French was heavily accented with German.

Was it only four years ago that Levi had felt troubled about the worldliness that was seeping into the church where he was a member? Then he heard about this "snow church," so-called because they were situated in a region where it snowed nine months out of a year. These people had migrated from Japan three hundred years earlier in search of religious freedom. Levi and his family paid these people a visit and were impressed by their warm, friendly fellowship and their level of spirituality. These people did no farming but made a living by hunting, fishing, and trapping. Their clothing was made from animal hides. They walked everywhere except when snow was on the ground, and then they made use of dog sleds. Their water for washing, cooking, and drinking was carried by hand from several springs. Levi and his family felt attracted to their rustic lifestyle. A year later, they moved there.

At first when Levi and his family attended their worship services, the ministers obligingly preached parts of the sermons in French. When his family continued to attend, the services reverted to Japanese. But during the week, these snow-church people of Japanese descent would gladly speak French to Levi and his family.

When Levi and his wife asked about being taken in as members, the ministry told them they would gladly take them in if they would put forth effort in learning Japanese. As time went on and their progress in learning Japanese was remarkably slow, the ministry reluctantly consented to take them in as members, provided they would continue their efforts to learn the language.

Three years later, Levi was sitting in a church service, listening to Bishop Miko preach. He could tell it was a moving message, but it could be understood only by those who knew Japanese well. While he could understand an occasional word, he could not understand enough to know what the sermon was about. How much he needed spiritual food for his soul! He still felt hungry after three years of receiving merely a pittance out of the church services every Sunday. To think that Bishop Miko and the rest of the congregation were every bit as fluent in French as in Japanese, yet they refused to provide his family with this accommodation.

Suddenly Levi could stand it no longer. He got up and escaped outside, where his emotions overtook him, and he stood there weeping.

Through his tears he glanced around and saw that not far away stood his wife, also weeping. Levi walked over and slipped his arm around her shoulders. They wept together. Finally they returned to the meeting room, feeling drained. This question weighed on their minds: *How can these people hurt us like this without even realizing it?*

By this time Levi had adapted to the culture, and the setting was an asset for maintaining spirituality and teaching their children. He liked it here, but he always felt left out on Sunday mornings.

Something else had recently started bothering him: the snow church's apathy toward outsiders and their unconcern for evangelizing. Occasionally other Canadians had attended Sunday morning services, but the sermons were still spoken in Japanese. Didn't the Bible teach that the Gospel was to be preached to all people? What could be a better way for French-speaking people to hear the Gospel than to sit in the services of the snow church? Yet what was the point of having outsiders attend if the services were in Japanese anyway? Was the snow church truly doing its evangelistic duty?

Much of this allegory was originally written by a French seeker who learned English with difficulty. He found the German even more difficult when he lived in several Old Order communities.[94] "Levi" and this French seeker represent a variety of people looking for a more meaningful and spiritual life. But the German language, however integral to our heritage, can easily become a hindrance and a stumbling block to seekers. What should we do to solve this dilemma?

An Attack or an Evaluation?

The main body of the Mennonite Church lost its distinctiveness and separation during the past century. And several generations ago, the liberal members eliminated numerous traditions. They failed to appreciate their heritage. After eliminating the time-tested traditions, they also questioned the fundamental principles. They professed enlightenment.

When I first began writing this book, I did not intend to attack any traditions of any plain groups. What a challenge to discuss these issues in a constructive way!

---

[94] *Plain Things,* March–April 2015, 23–24. The author's liberty added.

We agree that the German language is part of our heritage. But this raises questions when we relate to seekers. Are we being fair to potential converts to require them to learn our language to become a part of us?

Using English, however, raises another concern. Would switching to English in worship services open the door to more changes in our lifestyle and culture?

These are good questions, but they have no easy answers. I understand the concerns on both sides. We value the German language as a part of our heritage and culture. But it has erected a barrier in an English-speaking society. And most of us who speak German are every bit as fluent in English. Hence, we do not have a language barrier.

How would the exclusive use of German appear to us if we fully grasped God's love for mankind? The kingdom of Jesus Christ is not restricted to our traditional culture. We must, as Jesus has commanded, cross into different cultures to spread the Gospel of the kingdom. This includes crossing the line from our traditional German language to the language of the people we are trying to reach. This is part of the church's mandate in preaching the Gospel.

Adopting Another Language: Rebellion Against God's Order?

We might feel comfortable concluding that the reason we should keep the German is that God does not want everyone to speak one language. After Babel, the people naturally banded with those who spoke the same language. Would speaking English accelerate the tendency toward one language again? The English language is fast becoming a global language because of American trade and commerce with various nations.[95]

Is God displeased if we adopt the common language to be able to communicate with those who cannot understand ours? The reason God initiated language barriers was because of sin. As a result, even His chosen people are able to communicate with only a limited number of people, no matter how strong their vision is to spread the Gospel.

From one of the scattered tribes after Babel, God chose Abraham to carry on a religious line from which would descend the promised Messiah. The mother tongue of these Israelites was Hebrew. This was the language in which God's Word, the Old Testament, was written.

The Jews kept the Hebrew language until the Captivity. Then their mingling with foreign people jeopardized their mother tongue. When some Jewish men married foreign wives, their children no longer knew Hebrew.[96] By the time Jesus came to earth, Aramaic was the common language of the Jews.

The fact that Jesus spoke Aramaic is seen by several of His statements in the New Testament that were not translated. *Talitha cumi* (Mark 5:41), *Ephphatha* (Mark 7:34), and *Eli, Eli, lama sabachthani* (Matthew 27:46) are recognized by language scholars as Aramaic words.[97]

The fact that Jesus spoke Aramaic rather than Hebrew indicates that He was flexible in His use of language. Had the Jews spoken Greek, Jesus would have used that

---

[95] God can easily overrule in this matter.
[96] Nehemiah 13:24.
[97] *The Illustrated Manners and Customs of the Bible,* 345.

language. Had He been sent to the Germans, He would have used German, no matter if His mother tongue was Hebrew. Had He been sent to the English, He would have used English, even if His primary language was German. While it is not wrong to use the language of our heritage, we should not think it is the only language we should use.

The Tragedy of Babel Versus the Wonders of Pentecost

Aramaic was not the only language in use during this time. By the time of Jesus' crucifixion, Greek had gained prominence throughout the Roman Empire. Because God's message was intended as much for the Gentiles as for the Jews, the New Testament was written, not in the traditional language of the Jews, but in Greek, the common language of educated men in the Roman Empire.

Interestingly, the Jews were in a situation like our Old Order churches today. They had Hebrew, the language of their Old Testament, but it was no longer commonly spoken. It could be compared to High German for us. They spoke Aramaic in everyday life, as we speak Pennsylvania German. They had the Greek language for trade and commerce, much like English today.

Forty days after Jesus' resurrection, plus ten days after His ascension into heaven, signs and wonders occurred. A sound of a rushing wind descended, filling the entire house where the apostles and more than a hundred disciples were gathered. Cloven tongues like fire appeared, and the apostles and others began speaking in tongues.

This was a reversal of what had transpired approximately two thousand years earlier at Babel. Instead of making language barriers, the Lord miraculously enabled the disciples to speak in other languages so that the entire audience understood.

Both occurrences were marvelous acts of God. At Babel, God confounded the language because the people proposed to do evil. Several millennia later, God made it possible for people of diverse tongues to understand the message He spoke through the apostles, so that the Gospel could quickly spread to different nations of the world.

The apostles did not require the Gentile churches to learn Hebrew and Aramaic. God may have enabled the apostles to speak in tongues whenever He sent them to preach in regions where they did not know the language. Greek was a widely spoken language during that time. The apostles seemed fluent in that language. They likely did not speak in tongues if they knew the local language.

Why wasn't this gift of speaking in tongues preserved for future generations? We don't know. If we could use German exclusively and the non–Old Order people would understand, there would be no question which language to use.

Would God deem it appropriate to grant the gift of tongues if we have naturally acquired the language? Much false doctrine is spread by charismatic movements, which teach that if you can't speak in tongues, you don't have the Holy Spirit. Their speaking in tongues is different from the speaking in tongues at Pentecost during the transition between the Covenants. We should avoid charismatic doctrines.[98]

We should recognize, though, that God can enable someone to speak in tongues, as on the day of Pentecost, if that is His way of advancing His kingdom. In one instance, a conservative Mennonite bishop preached a sermon in English, and a woman in the audience who knew no English heard the message in French.[99] God can still use such marvels to communicate His Gospel, but He usually chooses not to. Instead, God has given people the ability to learn foreign languages so that they can preach the Gospel in other countries.

Beyond the Pentecostal Era

Another widely known language during the New Testament era was Latin. The superscription on top of Christ's cross was written in Latin, Hebrew, and Greek. Latin was the language adopted by the Roman Catholic Church. By the time the Anabaptist movement emerged, Latin was no longer a spoken language, but it was still used in the rituals of the Catholic Church.

The first Anabaptist leaders began teaching the common people in their language. The Bible was translated into several versions of German—Luther German and Froschauer German. To hear God's message preached in a language the common people could understand was a welcome change.

Today we are the descendants of those Anabaptists. We are reminded of who we are because we speak a dialect that

---

[98] 2 John 10.
[99] Lester Bauman, *Exploring the Book of Acts*, p. 17.

has survived many generations. But are we maintaining a Scriptural balance in the use of that dialect?

We are not opposed to speaking English. Living in an English-speaking society brings us into contact with people who cannot speak our language, so we must speak in their language to communicate with them. It would be disrespectful if someone talked to us in English, and we responded in our German dialect. Even when visiting informally in a group where all but one understand Pennsylvania German, English is the spoken language.

We wouldn't think of refraining from doing business (which is much less important than the Gospel) with English-speaking people until they learned our language. Even doing business through an interpreter would not be necessary, if we both know the same language. English is the language the government requires to be taught in all schools in the United States. And we recognize it as indispensable for the nation we live in. Except for the occasional German classes, all instruction in our Old Order schools is in English.

English is necessary for communication in secular dealings. Shouldn't this language be esteemed more important in our worship services? If it is discourteous to speak directly to an outsider person in our own language in an informal setting, how can we be so disrespectful as to do it in a worship setting? Shouldn't the spiritual be esteemed more highly than the secular?

Should we try to assist a seeker by communicating to him in his tongue outside of worship services? Certainly, a seeker needs more personal communication than merely attending our worship services. We have to wonder if our tradition of using German exclusively is the first sign to him that he can't fit in. How is the German language the first hindrance in discouraging a seeker? Generally a seeker needs time to sort through his perplexity and indecision. He is like a weak lamb needing nourishment. How can we give him that nourishment if we require him to learn German first? A seeker will want to attend our congregation for an indefinite time before he is ready to become part of us. He is already experiencing a radical adjustment by coming into another culture, and he does not want to make a hasty decision. Whether ready or not, early in his experience with us he is against a wall. We would like to help him make the necessary cultural adjustments when he's ready. But if we require German understanding first, he can't get that help.

This is where the exclusive use of German becomes a stumbling block. "Therefore if I know not the meaning of the voice, I shall be unto him that speaketh a barbarian [foreigner], and he that speaketh shall be a barbarian unto me" (1 Corinthians 14:11). Most seekers need time to adapt to our culture before committing themselves to it. We should expound to them the tenets of our faith at times other than in worship services. Yet God ordained preaching as the foundational method of providing spiritual teaching to mankind. Once seekers make up their minds, they might be willing to learn our language.

What about the transitional period before they decide to learn the language and adapt to our culture? At that time, they need spiritual instruction, and they need to hear it in a language they can understand. How can we make them feel welcome in our worship services if the ordained leaders are reluctant to speak in their language? Seekers need to know they are welcome in our worship services, and they would feel welcome if they could understand the service and the songs being sung. "I will sing with the spirit, and I will sing with the understanding also" (1 Corinthians 14:15).

Some ordained leaders do obligingly use some English if they are aware of someone in the audience who does not understand German. This is a respectful response to visitors. I appreciate the forbearance among Old Order ministers concerning differences of opinion about the use of German. This issue, however, could come to the forefront quite a bit more if we focus more on outreach.

Comparison of the Corinthian Tongues and German

Could we be as misguided in our use of the German language as the Corinthian church was in their abuse of speaking in tongues?[100] The apostle Paul corrected the church at Corinth for speaking in tongues. Unlike the tongues given by the Holy Spirit on the day of Pentecost, these tongues were not being translated by the Holy Spirit into the languages of the audience.[101] No wonder Paul said, "So likewise ye, except ye utter by the tongue words easy to be understood, how shall it be known what is spoken? for ye shall speak into the air" (1 Corinthians 14:9).

According to verses 23–25, are we not uncharitable if we

---

[100] 1 Corinthians 14.
[101] The word *unknown* has been added by the King James translators. Quite likely, few in the assembly knew these languages.

could use a language everyone knows, yet refuse to do so? "If therefore the whole church be come together into one place, and all speak with tongues, and there come in those that are unlearned, or unbelievers, will they not say that ye are mad?[102] But if all prophesy, and there come in one that believeth not, or one unlearned, he is convinced of all, he is judged of all: and thus are the secrets of his heart made manifest; and so falling down on his face, he will worship God, and report that God is in you of a truth."

If an unbeliever, especially one who mocks our religion, would sit in our services and hear a message preached in a language he does not understand, how would he be edified? And would he be ready to listen at some other time when we tried to explain the basic tenets of our faith and doctrines in his language?

More than sixty years ago, in a now-extinct Amish community , lived an older man who had often resisted the call of the Holy Spirit. Nonetheless, he respected the examples of his Amish neighbors—and the Amish bishop was a good friend of his. One day he heard the shocking news that the bishop had died instantly from a heart attack. This was a loud reminder to him that he too would not be on earth forever. His heart was softened. And since he had known the bishop well, he decided to attend the funeral.

It was a large funeral, with people from various states attending, both Amish and non-Amish. The funeral sermons were touching, soul-stirring messages; but—unfortunately—they could only be understood by those who knew German.

---

[102] The Greek word translated *mad* means "being out of one's mind."

Later, this old man earnestly said to the bishop's son, "If only I could have understood what those preachers were saying."[103] As is too often the case, the bishop's son did not realize until later this was an opportunity to explain the way of salvation while this old man's heart was receptive. Afterward, when someone did try to explain it to him, his heart was hardened again. In such a state, he died.

What can be more tragic than someone with a softening heart not being able to understand the message he so much needs? How can we be sure that his heart will still be soft later?

Certainly, there are language barriers we cannot help, and an interpreter may need to be summoned.[104] Language barriers are a hindrance in an age when God does not usually choose to give the gift of tongues. However, most Americans speak English fluently; therefore, the language barrier need not be there.

Other Factors to Consider

When we analyze history, it seems that some groups were too eager to drop the German language. After only one generation, some of their offspring no longer knew German. Once the transition was made to English, they no longer had to deal with language barriers and were able to put more effort into witnessing. If this in itself was not wrong, why did those in the "Old" Mennonite Church who adopted English eventually apostatize? Were they assimilated into the world because they accepted the English language as

---

[103] Elmer Schrock, *The Amish in the Shenandoah Valley*, 56–57.
[104] 1 Corinthians 14:27.

well as evangelistic outreach? Or was it because their hearts had drifted toward the world, and they disdained their heritage, including the German language? The same people who seemed to despise German tended to be eager to learn other languages so they could minister to people of other nations.

Before the division, the English language was a controversy. Not until the plain churches divided into Old Order and progressive faction, did the Old Order side require the German language as a landmark defining separation. But on what basis? Was it based on the immovable principles of God's Word? Or was it in reaction to the liberals and their use of English? As we discussed in the previous chapter, the basis for a tradition must be Biblical principles rather than merely the way our forefathers decided to do it. A tradition based on the Bible agrees with the spirit of the whole New Testament. Any tradition that overemphasizes one passage while de-emphasizing another is not based squarely on a Biblical foundation, even though the tradition in itself might not be wrong.

The language issue is a dilemma, seen as a choice between two "evils." Our forefathers' reluctance to drop the German probably did not stem from the belief that it was more sacred than English. Nor was it traditional stubbornness or sentiment. It likely stemmed from the fact that the writings of their faith and songs were in German. Many English writings at that time were by Protestant authors.

175

We have a wider variety of quality reading material available. No longer would dropping the German language sever ties with our written heritage. Today we have a large spectrum of reading material that embraces Anabaptist teachings. The majority of these books have been written in English.

This shift to English for reading material brought about partial illiteracy of the old German writings among the groups that have retained the spoken dialect. Although German is still our first language in communication, or the language we speak most fluently, it is no longer our first language for reading and writing. If German was still my first language for reading and writing, why am I writing this book in English? How many would read this book if it were written in German?

Many older Anabaptist writings formerly available only in the German or Dutch languages have been translated into English. Old books like the *Martyrs Mirror*, Menno Simons' and Dirk Philips' writings, and the Dordrecht Confession of Faith are now available in English. Most German-speaking Plain People in America find reading English to be easier than reading German.

Recently a hymnbook was published containing older English hymns and numerous English translations of German hymns. This book, *Still Waters Hymnal*, would qualify as an additional hymnbook for worship services, so that English-speaking people could sing with understanding. Many of these songs have meters that fit traditional tunes. This hymnbook has the potential to become a literary classic, embraced by those who value their heritage yet see a need for an English-language hymnbook.

This publication is only the beginning. Many more old German hymns could be translated into English without losing their deep meaning. Given enough time, these English translations would have the potential to become timeless classics.

Should We Drop the German?

What is wrong with knowing more than one language? It would be a blessing to know many more! My burden is that the German language would continue to be used, but not abused. To maintain the German, I hope that anyone who knows it will continue to practice it with those who are able to speak and understand it. I also desire that any German-speaking parents would pass the dialect on to their children. In the case of one parent knowing only English, and the other parent also knowing German, I see no reason why their children cannot learn both English and German at the same time. Children are bright and can easily learn more than one language at the same time.

I also advocate that the German language continue to be taught in our Christian schools. While German primers have their place, the focus should be on the terminology used in our old hymnbooks, Anabaptist writings, and the Luther translation of the Bible, rather than on terminology we are not likely to run across.

I like the grandeur of the Old German, but I am thankful when an English translation is at its side. I am privileged to be able to read the Luther German translation of the Bible because I can pick up alternate shades of meaning, which I would not receive by reading only the King James Version.

For German to be maintained, it needs to be taught from one generation to the next. That is good and must not be overlooked. And for the sake of those who have never learned it, we must keep our language in proper perspective. As we think of reaching out, we are not doing anyone a favor by pressuring someone to learn our language in order to be one of us. To make seekers feel welcome, we must use a language we can both understand. The German language may have a place in worship services, but not at the expense of those who cannot understand it.

To maintain the German and still accommodate seekers, perhaps we should consider both German and English services, with potential seekers being notified in advance which language will be used in the service that week. Any German services should have interpreters. Or we could follow the example of one Old Order church that designates the fifth Sunday of the month to be conducted in German, with interpretation provided. Alternate options could also be considered.

We want Christ's kingdom to be extended freely without obstructions or hindrances. Surely, under the Holy Spirit's direction, we can find a balanced position that can feed all of Christ's sheep.

Chapter Eleven

Evangelistic Outreach: A Recipe for Assimilation?

During the latter part of the nineteenth century, an "awakening" swept through Mennonite congregations, which included an awareness that Christians should be more active in mission work. More than one hundred years later, the original vision and activity has been lost. Today these branches of Mennonites are indistinguishable from Protestant churches, both in outward appearance and in theology.

When I went to school, one of my favorite subjects was mathematical equations. In a simple equation of $2 + n = 5$, simple arithmetic proves that $n = 3$. The sum of 2 and 3 equals 5.

Today, we have come up with another equation: the church + outreach = n. In this case, n equals assimilation. The older generation in the Old Order movements witnessed firsthand what befell the "higher" Mennonite Church conferences when they embraced evangelistic activity. Hence, it seemed safe to avoid evangelistic outreach at all costs.

But is the equation as simple as it sounds? Jesus' promise, "And, lo, I am with you alway, even unto the end of the world," is in context with His commission to go and preach the Gospel to all nations. According to this passage, we see that the church extends to all people, regardless of language, race, or culture. Outreach has been commissioned by Jesus Christ to build His kingdom. Why have some churches been assimilated into the world when they embraced outreach?

We don't know exactly how it all happens. What we do know is that Satan somehow succeeds in maneuvering things so that men misunderstand the truth of God's Word.

It's a long story, one that would make a book in itself. Briefly, however, the problem is a misunderstanding of Christ's kingdom. Where did the zeal come from? Did the Mennonites come to their conclusions from studying and applying the Bible? Or did they copy Protestant churches?

If history is to teach us anything, it is not to annul something that Christ has not annulled. Instead, shouldn't we be learning from history how not to make the same mistakes that others have?

Our challenge today is not to repeat the same mistakes. Therefore, we need to know what mistakes were made and how mission efforts were misguided.

Some Insights of Protestant Theology

As covered in Chapter 3, Protestant reformers such as Ulrich Zwingli and Justus Menius did not share an enthusiasm for evangelistic outreach. The Anabaptists were sometimes accused of "unauthorized" outreach. Not until the 1700s did stirrings for mission work arise among Protestants.

One historian, Theron Schlabach, writes,

> The motives of those who made up the nineteenth-century missionary movement were mixed. Missionary outreach went hand in hand with European, and especially British, imperialism.[105]

In plain English, this historian is saying that nineteenth-century missionaries taught natives the ways of the country from which they had come more than the Gospel of Jesus Christ. This mentality was also carried to America, where evangelizing meant teaching the natives the European culture. The missionaries were devoted to the wrong kingdom.

This same historian writes,

> Another motive surely was romanticism, as would-be missionaries suddenly heard calls to far-off continents, distant sea islands, and exotic peoples.[106]

Further, he says that other motives had to do with

---

[105] Schlabach, *Gospel*, 21.
[106] Ibid., 22.

humanitarianism, such as campaigns against slavery and other oppressive evils; or asceticism, such as afflicting oneself in order to achieve saintliness; or building a reputation. Schlabach notes,

> Love and compassion were apt to shade off into condescending attitudes of uplifting one's inferiors.[107]

According to Schlabach, while planting churches could have been the motives of some missionaries, the emphasis of the church sometimes got lost when missionaries became preoccupied with individual soul-saving. Some missionaries embraced eschatology because they felt the time was right that Christ would come back to establish an earthly kingdom. Interestingly, obedience to Christ's last commission was seldom expressed as a motive for evangelizing.

According to Protestant theology, evangelistic work largely meant going to foreign countries. It meant colonialism, teaching natives the culture of America or Europe. This was a major reason that some mission efforts were not sound.

There are differences between Anabaptist and Protestant theology. The Protestants were enemies of the Anabaptists in Europe, and they did not hesitate to persecute them. The introduction of Pietism, discussed in Chapter 3, brought more "spirituality" into Protestant churches. Eventually this produced a missionary zeal, which often seemed to be

---

[107] Ibid., 22.

interpreted as foreign missions.

Michael Martin writes that, in spite of their missionary zeal,

> Nearly all the churches promoted a worldly Christianity. Their religion went hand in hand with many carnal practices. . . . The camp meetings did some good, but politicians seeking supporters, salesmen, and young people looking for social fun also attended them. Because of these features, one historian described the meetings as part serious revival, part county fair, and part carnival.[108]

Further,

> From 1800–1900, Protestant churches grew dramatically, but had very little emphasis on discipleship. Membership and institutional growth was the measure of success; emphasis on repentance, instruction of new members, and church standards faded or disappeared.[109]

Another historian writes,

> As the Mennonites began to borrow from [American] revivalism, their understanding of salvation changed, yet they maintained their holy lifestyle. . . . Separation and nonresistance were absent in American revivalism. . . . As the Mennonites began . . . to promote their new

---

[108] Michael Martin, *Pilgrims and Politics*, 189.
[109] Ibid., 197.

programs (Sunday schools and mission work), they either ignored separation or they struggled with how to maintain separation with their new-found tools.[110]

Protestant theology emphasized that every soul we win adds a star to our heavenly crown, an idea that is not supported by the Scriptures.[111] This theology is reflected in songs such as "Winning Souls for Jesus," "Will There Be Any Stars?" and "Must I Go and Empty-Handed?" Such songs slowly and subtly can distort our thinking.

Some Mennonites in the latter part of the nineteenth century were influenced by Protestant thinking, and this affected their outreach endeavors. It is not fair to suppose that mission work in itself caused Mennonite apostasy. As one writer noted,

> Could it be more accurate, however, to realize that mission work was only a symptom of the loss of sound doctrine; that it was the error in doctrine that produced mission work and that finally resulted in complete apostasy?[112]

What mistakes did the liberal Mennonites of the late nineteenth and early twentieth centuries make in their mission efforts, which finally resulted in their assimilation into the world? Their greatest error was copying the Protestants, but what other mistakes did they make?

---

[110] Martin, *Joy*, 97.
[111] See Luke 17:10.
[112] Martin, "Misguided," 5.

What Really Happened?

In his book *Vision, Doctrine, War,* James C. Juhnke wrote:

> In its motivations and strategies Mennonite missionary renewal was more Protestant than Anabaptist. . . . Whereas sixteenth century Anabaptists had found their mission field within the boundaries of a Christendom they rejected, the Mennonites in the modern movement reached beyond a Christendom in which they were increasingly comfortable. As Mennonites now participated in the larger Protestant effort to carry the witness of Christendom to the far corners of the world, their traditional church/world dualism eroded. . . . For missionaries in Asia and Africa the differences between Mennonites and Protestants seemed less significant than the cultural gulf between pagan traditionalism and modern Western Christianity.[113]

This historian went on to explain how Mennonite missionaries learned methods through Protestant Sunday school literature, mission-society journals, Bible schools, and seminaries. Whenever they established a mission in a foreign country, they received assistance from Protestants who had already been on the field.[114]

Early on, some Mennonites became involved in Union Sunday schools, becoming yoked with a wide spectrum of

---

[113] Juhnke, *Vision,* 142.
[114] Ibid., 142.

denominations. As Theron Schlabach noted,

> "The highest, the proudest, and the dressiest classes" of Americans supported the Sunday School movement . . . They mixed Mennonites with "other societies," some of which taught "almost a worldwide way to heaven."[115]

These Sunday schools, held in cooperation with Protestant denominations, were instrumental in capturing a missionary vision.

These Protestant influences flowed through the hands of a few influential Mennonite men. John Funk grew up in eastern Pennsylvania and was highly educated. He moved to Chicago into a lumber business in 1857. There he was converted in a Presbyterian revival. He returned to Pennsylvania to be baptized and get married. Later he returned to Chicago, becoming active in Sunday school work in the same circle as Dwight L. Moody, an influential evangelist.

In 1864, Funk began to publish the *Herald of Truth*. In 1867, he moved to Elkhart, Indiana, and started a publishing company. Having been ordained a minister in 1865 and a bishop in 1892, he had a strong influence in conference meetings and on the printed page.

A publishing venture can be a good thing to promote Biblical conservative values. But it can also be a means to propagate liberal theology and propaganda. John Funk's publications carried much material from Protestant sources. The *Herald of Truth* was printed in German and English. The

---

[115] Schlabach, *Gospel*, 46–47.

German reflected the time-tested Anabaptist values, but the English material was heavily tainted with Protestant theology. Although the English language itself was not to blame, the eagerness of many Mennonites to embrace Protestant theology in the English language and to discard German carelessly should have raised a red flag.

Joseph Funk, a publisher in Virginia, wrote,

> The different denominations [should] lay aside their disputes about external things of minor importance and unite together to promote the redemption of Christ, by the spread of His glorious Gospel and the extension of His Kingdom from shore to shore.[116]

Joseph Funk was correct in saying that fulfilling Christ's last commission takes the cooperation of all true Christians. Yet he did not see the importance of remaining separate from denominations that lacked sound teaching. Likewise, two influential bishops in Virginia, Peter Burkholder and his son Martin, made the transition to English and occasionally preached in non-Mennonite churches.

Some who attended Dwight Moody's Bible Institute in Chicago brought "strange" doctrines back to the Mennonite fold, including premillennialism. When Mennonites opened their own colleges, Protestant doctrines came in. Then in some ordinations, brethren were selected from the ranks of those who had been seminary trained, instead of being selected by the traditional use of the lot. A basic education can be useful in the kingdom. But higher education both

---

[116] Ibid., 30.

within and without Mennonite circles seemed to produce a current that encouraged the Mennonite Church to adapt to Protestant ways. Members were chosen to go to foreign countries because they were highly educated, instead of being chosen through the voice of the congregation. Most importantly, higher education fostered individualism and distinctive classes in the "Old" Mennonite Church.

One factor in the failure of Mennonite missions may have been the way they chose when and where to start another mission outreach. Mennonites in Virginia in the 1860s were reaching out to mountain people in West Virginia. The mountain people invited preachers to conduct services and funerals. But these Virginia Mennonites did not consider this as mission work. To them, missions meant city and foreign work.

These outreach efforts resembled early Anabaptist outreach more closely than did later efforts. In the 1880s, Mennonites received an invitation to begin a mission outreach in southern Indiana. The response was unfortunate: those who promoted missions believed that there was more need in cities and among the foreign heathen than in rural areas in their own land. And the more-conservative Mennonites were not interested in becoming involved in any outreach.

During the nineteenth century, Protestant missions were often more independent than denominational. Some aspiring Mennonites sailed overseas or traveled into large cities under independent mission banners, rather than through moves overseen by Mennonites. The Chicago

Mission, begun by zealous youth, raised controversy among Mennonites. When a mission effort—like the Chicago mission—was not church-sponsored, some mission workers deviated from the standards of their home church. Motives for missions were sometimes mixed with political, rather than kingdom, aims. Solomon Ebersole lamented,

> [Without missions] this world is doomed to destruction. . . . We know that our cities rule the nation, and as our cities are, so our government will be.[117]

Institutionalism

A greater downfall of the late-nineteenth- and early-twentieth-century Mennonites was the influence of institutionalism: programs were organized complete with boards, committees, and the solicitation of funds for the work. Institutions in the form of mission boards, colleges, hospitals, mutual-aid societies, and retirement homes were established. What was meant to be a simple work of preaching and godly living became a series of complex organizations.

While institutions have their place for serving the needs of society, institutionalism, by its very nature, placed the Mennonites on a plane above the people they were trying to reach. As Mennonites focused on institutions, they departed from Jesus' concept of loving our neighbors. Sound Gospel preaching was replaced by social service. A social gospel

---

[117] Ibid., 49.

became evident.

Institutionalism influenced the Mennonites' view of those whom they were helping. In 1898, the progressive element in the Lancaster Conference began a mission for the blacks in the Welsh Mountain region. They built a mission station and attempted to teach the blacks a good work ethic. They established a stone quarry, a shirt factory, a broom-making shop, and farms for raising pigs and strawberries. Although the mission was an effort to teach the blacks good ethics, the attitudes of the Mennonites were condescending. An Illinois writer in the *Herald* in 1892 had commented,

The Mennonite church has been strictly a white man's church. The idea of a Negro or a Chinaman being a Mennonite . . . would make trouble, we being so dignified.[118]

We can't help wondering how the black people appreciated yielding to the Mennonites and being told what to do. Presenting the pure Gospel would have been the Scriptural way. The blacks' acceptance of the Gospel would eventually have produced good work ethics and moral values in ways that institutions themselves could not do.

This concept of institutionalism was also carried into foreign missions. After much discussion, in 1906, Mennonite missionaries in India purchased an eight-hundred-acre tract of land. "But what irony!" noted Schlabach.

> Mennonites, historically a humble and unassuming folk, were now in a lordly role. . . . The village was a unit of civil government . . . of a kind Mennonites' forebears had stoutly

---

[118] Ibid., 75.

rejected. Yet the missionaries defended their move. . . . Most of all, it would help give the emerging Christian community a solid economic base. That last argument the missionaries used also to defend industrial schools and other programs to teach orphans and other Christian youth various farming, business, and craft skills.[119]

Such an organization cost money—money the Mennonites did not have. They had to borrow at 12% interest. Can we imagine Jesus and the apostles organizing complex institutions and soliciting funds from the churches? The New Testament pattern reveals a simple mission structure: holding all things common, the rich sharing with the poor. Nowhere do we read that Jesus and the apostles begged for large sums of money to fund institutional missions.

A Protestant Understanding of Salvation—and Its Results

Another factor in the decline of the "Old" Mennonite Church was their tendency to separate ethics from salvation, and laying them on two different tracks. Protestants focused on an initial salvation experience, at the expense of the Biblical concepts of daily dying to self and maintaining one's salvation. Although many Mennonites upheld Bible doctrine and practice, they began to disconnect salvation from Christian living. This offered the impression of legalism. Some began to wonder: If externals don't save us, what's the

---

[119] Ibid., 95.

point of abiding by them?

This concept carried over to foreign missions. The natives were good Christians, even if they did not adhere to distinctive Mennonite practices. Mennonites on the mission field then decided that if the natives did not have to comply with these "extras," missionaries didn't need to either. This affected members in the home congregations, who reasoned that "if the members on the mission field don't have to comply with the standards, we don't have to comply with them at home either."

Some missionaries fellowshipped with non-Mennonite missionaries on foreign soil. To do so seemed natural, since they were there through the influence of other denominations. Missionaries were sorely tempted to participate in communion at non-Mennonite communion services. In east Africa, it became common for Mennonite missionaries to commune with non-Mennonite missionaries.[120]

In spite of their original focus on city and foreign missions, Schlabach noted that by the 1930s, Mennonites began to accept that every congregation was a mission post. More and more outreach was dedicated to serving needs closer to home. Some of these home-based outreach programs were more in line with the Scriptures and the pattern of the early Anabaptists. Nevertheless, Mennonite outreach activity seemed to have slacked off by the 1950s, just prior to their being assimilated into the larger culture.[121]

This raises a question. Did the Mennonites lose their zeal

[120] Ibid., 150.
[121] Ibid., 227.

for outreach when they were assimilated? If so, mission outreach was not to blame for the apostasy during the 1950s and 1960s. Rather, it would seem that energy for outreach ebbed as the church was assimilated. If this was indeed the case, it casts doubt on the theory that evangelistic outreach is a gateway to assimilation.

Ecumenism and Its Tragic Results

Institutional activity continued. After World War II, the Mennonite Central Committee (MCC) expanded its program. Other relief and service agencies emerged, offering Mennonites a channel for service as well as new opportunities for adventure, glamour, and activism. While relief and service have their place, they are not substitutes for presenting the Gospel. Furthermore, MCC was an ecumenical effort. Not only did it cooperate with various denominations of Plain People, but it also opened the door for more association with Protestants.

Overall, the mid-twentieth-century Mennonites, other than the Old Order segment, were willing to cooperate with other denominations in pushing for worldwide unity at the expense of time-tested values. As a result, they became detached from their Scriptural moorings of separation and distinctiveness. I quote William McGrath:

> The next most destructive influence on the churches [that] descended from the Anabaptists, came with the Ecumenical movement and the formation of the World Council of churches in 1948. The thrust of the

Ecumenical movement was to bring together the many different denominations into one world church organization. The method used was to emphasize the social gospel of relief, service, and international socialism. The slogan used was "doctrine divides, service unites."[122]

Evangelistic outreach, therefore, was *not* the destructive factor leading to the assimilation of the Mennonite Church. Ecumenism was to blame. The Mennonites' cooperation with denominations that did not practice nonresistance and non-conformity had a negative impact on the traditional stand of the Mennonite Church. If Protestants and Catholics could be Christians without distinctiveness, why shouldn't it also work for Mennonites?

No wonder the "Old" Mennonite Church apostatized! Certainly, not all was bad about these mission efforts, which were based on ecumenical principles rather than on a Scriptural foundation. Quite likely, some souls found salvation who otherwise might not have. Nevertheless, it was a tremendous loss for Mennonites who were once plain and conservative.

Perhaps we could summarize this phase of history by quoting Theron Schlabach one more time:

> Had they listened to stiller, smaller sounds, they might have gone forth not quite so much to the drumbeat of Anglo-American Protestantism, and therefore less in step with the West's larger march of energetic

---

[122] William McGrath, *Christian Discipline*, 37.

imperialism. Had they listened more to Jesus' low-key rhythm, to the modest congregations of Christians of Paul's time, to the Anabaptists, to the best words of their Mennonite fathers— ah, but what was, was. The drumbeat was next to deafening. And its rhythm did call Mennonites to mission.[123]

Loss of Vision

In light of the apostasy of many mission-minded churches, is it any wonder that many plain groups have been wary of evangelizing?

The Russian Mennonites had promised not to evangelize outside their own circles. But the Anabaptists who migrated to America faced no such restrictions. Nevertheless, evangelistic outreach was not their reason for migrating to America.

Those who migrated believed in the same basic teachings of their forefathers. They appeared to be a religious, devout people, and they continued the form of worship they had been used to, which they could practice without fear. Their children knew only about the freedom of living in America.

Prior to the Industrial Revolution, the colonists in America had largely been self-sufficient, growing their own food and making their own clothing. What they could not produce, they did without or bartered with each other by exchanging goods. Only the extremely wealthy could afford a luxurious lifestyle.

The Industrial Revolution brought mass-produced goods

---

[123] Schlabach, *Gospel,* 52–53.

at affordable prices. This change was not wrong in itself, but it had a profound effect in shifting society toward materialism. The plain groups were not exempt.

Meanwhile, Anabaptist church life had drifted into formalism. Some young people, like starving sheep, left their heritage. Some were seeking for more spirituality, but others left because they wanted more liberty. Many young people delayed joining the church until after marriage.

Furthermore, young people were being educated in English and not all could read the Old German writings and hymns. The older people knew German but could not read English. Their books contained sound writings by their Anabaptist forefathers, whereas the English books contained a Protestant flavor.

The nineteenth-century plain churches needed a revival. The Mennonite Church had failed to make its members, especially young people, feel secure and needed. In light of this, men like John Funk had good ideas and a noble vision. The Sunday schools and evangelistic meetings that sprang up among Mennonites could have been positive had they been church-sanctioned innovations instead of self-appointed ventures. As it was, these organized activities did help to keep young people in the Mennonite Church. But in the end, the whole Mennonite body was absorbed into Protestantism except for a conservative remnant.

These changes in the Mennonite Church were part of the "great awakening," which affected many American churches. It eventually resulted in the Old Order groups separating from the progressive elements. Like many divisions, seldom is one side always right while the other side is completely wrong.

In these Old Order/liberal divisions, it seems both sides stubbornly persisted in clinging to their viewpoints and were not open to consider the insights of the other side. Had both sides been willing to discuss their differences in a peaceable manner, they could have learned from each other and eventually come up with a solution that was satisfactory to both sides. Had the plain churches been willing to regain the vision that had initiated the Anabaptist movement in the first place, they could have worked together toward true Biblical revival. The liberals could have listened to the conservatives' concerns and applied the brakes to their progressivism. The conservatives too could have seen the advantages and benefits of the liberals' evangelistic viewpoint and the need for reaching out.

Unavoidably, the true church will sometimes face pressure to change. Change is not always wrong. But the principles that identify the true church never change, because these principles are based on the Bible. The applications, however, which are based on these principles, will vary from one congregation to the next, from one generation to the next, and from one culture to the next. We can't ignore the presence of change by clinging to the past. This has the potential to create a cold formalism that can be mistaken for Biblical faithfulness.

Since English is the prevalent American language, it would have seemed logical to write new English books and songs based on the old Anabaptist theology and to translate into English the old German books and songs that the conservatives appreciated so much. Conservatives overreacted when they refused to acknowledge a place for the English language in an English-speaking society. They felt that adhering to the German language would prevent them from being assimilated into the world.

The liberals, however, were too eager to change their position. They were quick to drop their Old German Anabaptist writings and completely adopt English writings with a Protestant flavor. They did not seem to realize what they would lose when they switched over to English.

What Can We Learn?

What can we learn from this phase of Mennonite history? How can we safeguard our plain churches so that we do not make the same mistakes of the liberal Mennonites?

To avoid evangelistic outreach because of the way the liberal Mennonites practiced it is overreaction. Further, as was pointed out earlier, the Anabaptist groups migrating to America had lost their evangelistic zeal while they were living in Europe. After several generations of little evangelistic activity, it is no wonder that evangelistic outreach seemed to them as something new. They had forgotten that it was an important part of their heritage.

We must recognize that our influential forefathers who initiated the Old Order movement were not perfect. We must focus on their strengths and grant grace to their failures. We do not gain anything by reproaching them.

To return to the equation presented at the beginning of this chapter, we must add another factor to arrive at a fair analysis. For the liberal element, it was not "the church + outreach = assimilation." But it was "the church + a Protestant foundation + outreach = assimilation." By contrast, a better equation is "the church + a Scriptural foundation + outreach = an obedient body of believers, separate and peculiar, with a vibrant vision for God's kingdom."

To regain this vision for sound, Biblical outreach, we must look beyond the era of nineteenth-century Protestantism. Where the stream has been polluted, we must go back to the source of the spring, from whence flows pure, clear water. Only then can God bless our outreach endeavors.

The influences that plain churches faced in the nineteenth century are still real today. We need clear teaching and warning. The line between Anabaptists and Protestants was more distinct when the Protestants persecuted the Anabaptists. Today, in a political climate of religious freedom, this boundary is less distinct, and it seems pointless to try to evangelize Protestants. (The liberal Mennonites did not do that. They associated with the Protestants.) However, if other groups have an unbiblical understanding in areas such as Christ's kingdom, separation, nonresistance, and salvation, we have a duty to enlighten them.

How Can We Prevent History from Repeating Itself?

During the 1950s and 1960s, a conservative remnant withdrew from the liberal Mennonite body. They formed new conference and fellowship groups, determined to regain principles that had become lost in the conferences they had left. One thing did not change: their mission activity.

Today, fifty years later, these churches are still active in evangelistic outreach. Will history repeat itself? Will these conservative Mennonite churches be assimilated into Protestantism within another twenty to fifty years?

As was mentioned earlier in this chapter, it was not mission work in itself that caused apostasy in the "Old" Mennonite Church. Rather, it was the shift in doctrine.

For this, we cannot blame evangelistic outreach. Because the church was building on a Protestant foundation rather than on a Biblical one, it is understandable that the church became Protestant in appearance after a few generations. Their mission outreach reflected Protestant theology as a result. And it took about seventy years until the fruits were fully mature.

How can we maintain sound outreach practices today so that history does not repeat itself? Since Christ has authorized evangelistic outreach, it is reasonable to think that if the rest of our doctrines are sound, our mission efforts will be sound as well.

What, then, are some warning signs or indications that a church and its outreach efforts are apostatizing?

- Do they believe that salvation is a one-time experience? Do they place Christian living and salvation on separate tracks? Are they under the impression that their status in heaven is greater if they put in effort in active mission work? Do they look critically at churches that do not actively evangelize?

- Are their evangelistic efforts individualistic rather than church-centered? Do individual members resent the church? Do they pursue evangelistic work under a banner that is not their local church?

- Do they view mission work exclusively as a separate work away from home in some large city or foreign country? Does their mission work involve teaching people in foreign countries the American culture? Are their aspirations romantic, idealizing that the only worthy work is far away from home?

- Are they involved in interdenominational Sunday schools? Do they work closely with other denominations that do not share their values? Do they include churches that tolerate divorce, remarriage, participation in war, and other vices that the Bible condemns? Do they exchange Protestant or Catholic preachers in their pulpits? Do they work with Protestants on the mission field? Do they prove to be ambassadors of America rather than of Christ?

- Do they view higher education as necessary in becoming an effective missionary? Do they attend Protestant colleges? Do they select ministers and missionaries from the seminary-trained ranks?

- Are their institutions independent, complex organizations that compete with the church, rather than complementing it? Do they publish writings without having them reviewed for doctrinal soundness?

If conservative churches can answer "no" to the questions above, they are avoiding the pitfalls that have led many others to apostasy.

In essence, much of what is called mission work today is the result of men building their own kingdom rather than Christ's. As was discussed in Chapter 8, our focus must not be on lifestyle or outreach. Our focus must be on the kingdom of Christ. We must maintain sound doctrine at all costs, lest history repeat itself. That includes our mission efforts. Unless sound doctrine is taught and practiced in every generation, it will be lost.

Where would the "Old" Mennonite Church be today if it could have answered "no" to these questions? The successes and failures of this segment of God's people are buried in the ashes of history. Today it is up to us to maintain the faith. Christ has entrusted us with a commission. We must not fail Him.

Chapter Twelve

To Build a Bridge

We come to the final chapter on evangelistic outreach—or we could say, reaching out with the Gospel. A bridge is a beautiful picture of reaching across and going to others with the Gospel. A bridge also pictures us reaching out to our brothers as we share with them in our congregations. Building bridges illustrates godliness. Consider how Jesus built a bridge when He came down to live and die so that mankind could be reconciled to God. Let us be bridge builders.

In Chapter 3, we discussed how the Scriptural segment of Anabaptists endeavored to obey the Scriptures, no matter what the cost. We especially focused on their commendable zeal for evangelizing, no matter how much opposition they faced.

The Anabaptists were not perfect. They had their faults and were not without divisions. History shows that not all was right, even in times of persecution. Those hard times did not bring about a utopian church life. We can learn from history, because we face some of the same influences today. Satan is still endeavoring to splinter God's church.

The most Scriptural segment of Anabaptists did not compromise. But as mentioned in Chapter 3, the Anabaptist movement was diverse. Not every group represented a Scriptural church. But since they rebaptized converts to their groups, the authorities labeled them as Anabaptist. Some of these groups were led by zealous, evangelistic, radical leaders who taught extreme interpretations of prophecy. They were not all nonresistant. During this era of the late 1520s through the 1530s, some dissension existed among the Anabaptists.

Out of one of the radical movements, Dutch Anabaptism was born. Obbe Philips and his brother Dirk recognized that according to the Bible, they had been deceived by Melchior Hofmann's vengeful teachings. They withdrew and began a more Scriptural church. Menno Simons joined them soon afterward.

By studying the Bible, the Philips brothers and Menno Simons recognized the need for maintaining a pure church, consisting only of regenerated believers who obeyed the whole Bible. No longer could they recognize these radical Anabaptists as brethren. That meant they needed to shun them so that their influence would not permeate the true church.

Out of this upheaval, the Dutch Anabaptist view of shunning emerged, which differed from the Swiss

To Build a Bridge

Anabaptist view. The Dutch Anabaptists became zealous to maintain purity in the church. They recognized the church's responsibility to excommunicate and shun those whose lives gave evidence of sin. But what makes a pure church? On this question, the Dutch Anabaptists did not agree with each other.

In 1556, conflict emerged on how the ban should be applied. Leenaert Bouwens required that Swaen Rutgers shun her husband, which according to the Dutch Anabaptist interpretation of shunning meant she could no longer eat or live with him. She refused to comply with this strict order. Menno Simons was more lenient; he thought it would not be necessary—not between husband and wife!

This became the first major division in Anabaptist history where brethren separated from each other, rather than removing themselves from an unscriptural group. The group with the more lenient position on the ban and shunning became known as the Waterlanders.[124]

In spite of this disharmony, the groups did not ban and shun each other. They merely separated into two fellowships. Around ten years later, another major division occurred in the original Dutch Anabaptist group. Because of persecution, many Dutch Flemish Anabaptists had moved north and settled in the region of the Dutch Frisian Anabaptists. Because of their separate history, these groups varied culturally.

It is beyond the scope of this writing to go into detail as to the cause of the split. The original issues were soon

---

[124] Dyck, *Introduction*, 123–125; Martin, *Cup and Cross*, 142; Horsch, *Mennonites*, 236.

forgotten. But the friction between both sides continued. They began using the ban and shunning each other in a spirit of revenge, thereby warping its Scriptural function. Members transferring from one group to the other were rebaptized.[125]

This was not the only split. When a piece of wood is split once, it becomes easier to split again. And again. And when the Dutch Anabaptists split, too often both sides banned and shunned each other as enemies.

It's not that the Dutch Anabaptists never sought to heal these splits. Over the next years, they pursued various attempts to reunite. In 1632, leaders representing different factions met at Dordrecht to draw up a confession of faith in an effort to unify the various groups. This gathering bore some good fruit, although the Dutch Anabaptists were never completely reunited.

The Painful Conflict of the 1690s

This brings us to the Jacob Ammann era and the painful conflict of the 1690s. In 1660, the Dordrecht Confession was accepted by some of the Swiss Anabaptists, particularly in the Alsace region of France.[126] As a result, they accepted the Dutch Anabaptist view on shunning.

And then, for the first time in their history, the Swiss Anabaptists would divide. Jacob Ammann, a bishop of the

---

[125] Lehman, *Russian,* 21.

[126] In his book *Unser Leit,* Leroy Beachy concludes that the Mennonites in Alsace, referred to as Oberlander, and the Mennonites in Switzerland, referred to as Emmenthaler, were actually two culturally distinct groups. (His conclusion makes sense because of the different surnames we find among the Amish, versus the Mennonites.) The Oberlander were more evangelistic than the Emmenthaler—their group consisted of many converts from the Reformed churches. Thus the Amish already existed before the 1690s, but were not formally called by that name until after 1693 and their separation from the Reist side.

Alsace churches, concluded that some serious backsliding had occurred during the previous decades. Evidently, some Swiss Anabaptist leaders had become lax in church discipline. By this time, some Swiss brethren were compromising aspects of their faith by occasionally attending the services of the state churches and giving consent for their babies and children to be baptized in order to escape persecution more easily.[127]

Ammann viewed this tolerance as a serious compromise and drift from what the Anabaptists had initially stood for. He concluded that something needed to be done.

As bishop, Ammann found support among like-minded leaders in his circle of congregations in the Alsace region. Then he traveled to congregations in Switzerland to convince those congregations to accept his views. His foremost concern was the lax way the Swiss brethren practiced the ban and shunning.

The trouble came to a head when Ammann met with an elderly bishop, Hans Reist. Reist, it is said, could not accept Ammann's views and opposed him. Many of the Swiss brethren supporting Reist withstood Ammann.

What happened that year was a tragedy that could have been avoided had Ammann used foresight. As is usually the case in church splits, both sides were at fault in this 1693 confrontation. Ammann called a meeting, only to hear a rebuttal from Reist and his fellow ministers. Several weeks later at another meeting, Reist failed to show up. When messengers were sent out to apprehend him, Reist refused

---

[127] John D. Roth, trans., *Letters of the Amish Division: A Sourcebook*, 5; Martin, *Cup and Cross*, 105.

to come, saying that it was harvest time. Whereupon Ammann excommunicated Reist, which of course did not relieve the tension. Several others expressed their disagreement and were promptly excommunicated. One woman pled with Ammann not to act so rashly. This did nothing to appease Ammann's anger. [128]

Ammann sent letters to various churches throughout Switzerland, stating that if the members did not agree with him by a certain date, they would also be excommunicated. [129] The division deepened, with the majority of the churches in Alsace identifying with Ammann, and most of the churches in Switzerland identifying with Reist.

Some of those involved on both sides of the division were troubled by what was done. In time, various attempts were made at reconciliation. Jacob Ammann and some of his fellow ministers admitted they had acted too rashly, and they placed themselves in the ban. [130] But they still insisted that their view of the ban and shunning be kept. Neither side could tolerate the difference in application. Thus the division remained permanent.

Walls That Divide

A father and his sons purchased a farm with a wide, deep river winding through the middle. On the side opposite the buildings lay many acres of productive land. But it was overgrown with brush because there was no easy

---

[128] Roth, *Letters*, 22.
[129] Ibid., 25–26.
[130] Ibid., 26; William McGrath, *The Mystery of Jacob Ammann*, 56.

way to cross the wide river.

Along the river's banks lay heaps of rocks. Occasional floods washed more rocks ashore into the low-lying fields beside the river. One of the sons, whose talent lay in masonry, proposed picking up those rocks and using them to build a bridge. After much labor, a strong, sturdy bridge spanned the river. The construction was not without its hurdles and setbacks, but by patiently working together and persevering, they finally accomplished what needed to be done. After more months of work, the fertile lands on the far side of the river brought forth a rich harvest.

This allegory is an illustration of what is happening in our plain churches today. It took working together to build the bridge. Had this young man's father and his brothers withstood him, he could not have accomplished this alone. And without the bridge, they could not have developed the farm's potential.

Relationships with our brethren in the faith can sometimes seem like an impassable river. It may be tempting to throw the rocks at each other or to use them to construct walls. Herein lies the true test: Do we truly love our brethren? Or do we justify our enmity against each other?

True Christians will occasionally have disagreements. We tend to defend our own views and to despise others who see a matter differently. We have to be on guard because Satan is trying to destroy relationships. We need each other as a brotherhood, where different views and opinions can blend. Therefore, we need to respect and appreciate the insights of others, and to realize that our way of viewing something is not the only way.

In the Book of Acts, we read of the unity of the early Christian church. "The multitude of them that believed were of one heart and of one soul" (Acts 4:32). This produced a collective witness to unbelievers. So united were these early believers that they voluntarily sold their possessions and gave to those who lacked. They held all their things in common.

Various passages in the Epistles emphasize the need for unity. For example, the apostle Paul wrote to the Corinthians, "Now I beseech you, brethren, by the name of our Lord Jesus Christ, that ye all speak the same thing, and that there be no divisions among you; but that ye be perfectly joined together in the same mind and in the same judgment" (1 Corinthians 1:10). To the Philippians, he wrote, "Let us walk by the same rule, let us mind the same thing. Brethren, be followers together of me, and mark them which walk so as ye have us for an ensample" (Philippians 3:16–17). He warned the Romans, "Now I beseech you, brethren, mark them which cause divisions and offences contrary to the doctrine which ye have learned; and avoid them" (Romans 16:17). And he warned the Corinthians, "For ye are yet carnal: for whereas there is among you envying, and strife, and divisions, are ye not carnal, and walk as men?" (1 Corinthians 3:3). "For first of all, when ye come together in the church, I hear that there be divisions among you; and I partly believe it" (1 Corinthians 11:18).

The apostle Peter wrote these words: "Finally, be ye all of

one mind, having compassion one of another, love as brethren, be pitiful, be courteous" (1 Peter 3:8). The Luther German states this verse more forcefully. Translated, it says, "Finally then, be (ye) altogether like-minded, compassionate, brotherly, merciful, (and) friendly."

If we were compassionate, brotherly, merciful, and friendly toward our brethren, there would be less strain in our relationships. There would be fewer church splits. But how is that possible as long as imperfect mortals live together, and not everyone views every issue the same way? When we have disagreements with our brethren, are we disobeying these New Testament commands?

Noted for Division

Some non-plain scholars have observed that too often the plain churches are noted—not for love, peace, and unity— but rather for bickering, strife, and divisions. We acknowledge that some Protestant churches have laid aside denominational differences in favor of unity. But some of this is an ecumenical unity rather than a Scriptural unity. And thus, they have lost Scriptural principles. Unity is never Scriptural when Bible principles are compromised. Satan and his demons are also united.

It is shameful to admit, but many churches have divided when instead they might have come to a peaceful solution by sitting down and listening to each other. This is much better than fighting with fellow brethren. Too often, however, emerging factions regard the other side as an enemy. That is exactly what Satan wants.

We can't help wondering what our plain churches would

be like today if Ammann and Reist, along with their respective supporters, had been open to the other side's views. The final reconciliation attempt seems to have failed because of their disagreement on how strongly the ban and shunning should be applied. This was not a matter of compromising a solid, Biblical principle. Rather, it was a disagreement in the application. The Emmenthaler had been practicing a softer ban all along. They were not losing out in their beliefs about the ban, as Ammann too readily supposed. Both sides should have respected each other's differences and continued their fellowship with each other. They certainly could have learned from each other. For too long, both sides hated each other. Even the Reist side banned the Ammann side, despite their belief in a less rigorous application of the ban.

More than thirty years ago, *Family Life* published an article called "The Walls That Divide Us." This article has recently been published in booklet form. It includes a few more articles written by several authors which address a blight that has overtaken our plain churches. The booklet points out similarities between church splits and divorce, making this thought-provoking observation:

> Both [divorce and church splits] pave the way for more. Once divorce becomes accepted in a nation or a church, the rate will zoom up and up. Why? Because when that option does not exist, troubled spouses continue to seek some solution. If they know of other couples who have gone the divorce route, and they know

they have that choice, they will not try as hard to make their marriage work. As a result, fewer marriages will work. The same is tragically true of churches. Every time a piece of wood is split, the easier it is to split it again. Every time a church yields to division, the easier it is to do so next time.[131]

This could be one reason that the church is so weak in resisting evil. The more a church splinters into non-fellowshipping factions, the weaker it becomes. There is more strength in a collective body of believers fighting against evil than in one individual fighting alone. "United we stand; divided we fall."

Someone may ask, Is a division that is instigated in tumult different from a peaceful reorganization? As was mentioned in Chapter 9, the church was not organized under one culture, perspective, standpoint, or *Ordnung* during New Testament times. For this reason, the apostle Paul addressed the painful reality that some differences need to be respected and tolerated. In spite of the New Testament emphasis on unity, we must accept that there will be differences among God's people. As long as these differences do not erode the foundation of the Gospel, Jesus Christ, we must respect them.

Let There Be No Strife

Consider the account of Abraham and Lot. Both of them possessed large herds of cattle and flocks of sheep and

---

[131]Anonymous, *The Walls That Divide Us,* 28.

goats—so many that a shortage of grazing land developed. The Bible says there was strife between Abraham's herdsmen and Lot's herdsmen.[132]

However, Abraham desired that there be no contention. "And Abram said unto Lot, Let there be no strife, I pray thee, between me and thee, and between my herdmen and thy herdmen; for we be brethren" (Genesis 13:8). Then Abraham made a generous offer to Lot and told him that he could have first choice.

Here we observe a peaceful separation. Although Abraham and Lot separated physically and organizationally, they still esteemed each other as brethren. And when God told Abraham that Sodom and Gomorrah would be destroyed, Abraham remembered Lot and interceded to God for the righteous. Abraham displayed true brotherly love toward his nephew. Therefore, this separation was not a split, because Abraham and Lot still viewed themselves as brethren, in spite of their differences. Yet reorganization seemed necessary under the circumstances.

Not all reorganization in history, though, has been peaceful. After King Solomon's death, the Israelites went through a turbulent division. Solomon's son Rehoboam, king of Judah, chose 180,000 warriors to fight against Israel and take the kingdom back into his hands by force. But God intervened. "The word of the LORD came to Shemaiah the man of God, saying, Speak unto Rehoboam the son of Solomon, king of Judah, and to all Israel in Judah and Benjamin, saying, Thus saith the LORD, Ye shall not go up,

---

[132] Genesis 13:7.

nor fight against your brethren: return every man to his house: for this thing is done of me" (2 Chronicles 11:2–4).

In spite of God's warning, "There were wars between Rehoboam and Jeroboam continually" (2 Chronicles 12:15). When Rehoboam died, his son Abijah reigned. The conflict continued. In 2 Chronicles 13, we read how Abijah chose 400,000 men, and Jeroboam chose 800,000 men to fight against each other. This civil war did not go as planned. Abijah stood on Mount Zemaraim and told Jeroboam and all Israel not to fight, for they would not succeed. God had promised the kingdom to David, but Jeroboam had taken it away by force.

And then Israel had fallen into idolatry and forsaken the Lord. Judah too had deviated from God's Law, but not to the extent that Israel had.

There was a horrible battle, and God reached down and delivered Jeroboam and his men into the hands of Judah. Five hundred thousand men of Israel were killed for resisting their fellow brethren of Judah.

The above account is not pleasant reading, but it is recorded "for our admonition" (1 Corinthians 10:11) so we don't make a similar mistake. The lesson is plain! We cannot harbor resentment against any part of God's people and expect God's blessing to rest upon us. If we do, we are in the wrong, even if the other side has unresolved issues. We are commanded to love our enemies; how much more, then, our brethren! As defenseless people, we must not oppose our fellow brethren, be they of our own brotherhood or of a congregation that has a different standard of practice.

If we backbite our brethren, whoever they may be, we are not nonresistant. There never has been a war anywhere in the world that did not start with opposing sides degrading each other. In the world, it is understandable that there are wars. But we in the church know better! If strife among God's people is not hatred, what is it? Further, a lack of love is also hatred, because the opposite of love is hate! The New Testament makes it plain that "Whosoever hateth his brother is a murderer: and ye know that no murderer hath eternal life abiding in him" (1 John 3:15).

Christ's Prayer for Unity

The seventeenth chapter of St. John records a heartfelt prayer that Jesus prayed to His Father. His foremost concern was for the unity of the believers. In this world, His followers would be sorely tested, and the world would hate them. But Jesus prayed, "That they all may be one; as thou, Father, art in me, and I in thee, that they also may be one in us: that the world may believe that thou hast sent me" (John 17:21).

What did Jesus have in mind when He prayed these words? And was His prayer not answered, when we consider the different denominations consisting of various Christians who do not fellowship with each other?

No. For when true Christians in any group love their Lord, they obey His teachings. This draws them together with other believers in the Spirit, though not necessarily organizationally. Furthermore, the New Testament leaves some room for differences. "Now there are diversities of gifts, but the same Spirit. And there are differences of administrations, but the same Lord. And there are diversities of operations, but it is the same God which worketh all in all" (1 Corinthians 12:4–6). I understand this passage to mean that some differences in application are acceptable among congregations and affiliations within the body of Christ. Furthermore, if the Christian church worldwide was intended to be as one organizationally (i.e., adhering to the same culture, *Ordnung,* etc.), why did the apostle Paul write Romans 14, which teaches accepting those who think differently?

Was this the failure of the Frisian and Flemish factions of Anabaptists, who could not tolerate differences in each other? Did they each view themselves as the one true church, and could they not see the other side as being part of the one true church as well?

Ammann seems to have viewed his own group as the one true church.[133] On the other hand, Reist's group felt that they, along with Ammann's group, the truehearted Halfway Anabaptists, and Christians in other groups, all composed the one true church.

Reist and his followers may have been too open-minded. But Ammann and his followers did not seem open-minded enough to consider that the Reist group might be a part of the one true church. After the division, it was logical for Ammann's side to conclude that since there was only one true church, and since their side was maintaining the truth more closely, they must be it.

However, the one true church is not restricted to one

---

[133] Roth, *Letters,* 24.

denomination, nor is the ban to be applied toward those who merely disagree with us. Had the Dutch Anabaptists and Jacob Ammann applied the ban according to Matthew 18:15–17 and 1 Corinthians 5, instead of misusing it, history would probably be different.

I am not implying that since we respect and appreciate the positions of other church groups, we should formally fellowship with them. The oneness that Christ so fervently desires is that the true church worldwide would be unified in its vision, purpose, and Scriptural obedience. Such a union would become an irresistible witness to the world. Scriptural evangelizing methods would be more effective as well.

In this sense, all self-denying and cross-bearing Christians worldwide should be considered our brethren and sisters in the faith, not only those within our affiliation. I come to this conclusion because these are the souls we will meet in heaven, if by God's grace and our obedience we are there. If we will see each other in heaven, shouldn't we get along with each other on earth?

Naturally, we will feel a closer relationship with our brethren and sisters in our local congregation and fellowship. That is the way it should be. There should always be more like-mindedness in a local congregation than is ever possible in the universal church. Too many major differences in a local congregation can wreck its stability and strength.

Satan's Determination

In summary, the question of whether we should be

involved in evangelistic outreach has the potential to generate strife, animosity, confusion, and division. Satan is determined to see that it happens. If we oppose our fellow brothers and sisters because of our differences, we have not learned from history. We will then be repeating the history of Jacob Ammann and the Dutch Anabaptists.

When a community or a denomination has irreconcilable differences, does that indicate they have fallen from God's grace? I don't think so. We are human; therefore, differences will arise between brethren, which may seem impossible to reconcile.

We can learn to appreciate and respect different opinions and applications. Differences within a congregation can damage its stability. But a mutual agreement for peaceful reorganization, with one faction relocating geographically and both sides esteeming each other as brethren, will go a long way in maintaining unity. To be divided organizationally and geographically does not necessarily mean to be divided spiritually. We have no Scriptural grounds to fall out with our brethren who see matters differently from us, let alone to ban or shun them.

Our calling is to build bridges, not walls. For too long, our plain churches have built walls around their own fortresses. They fear that reaching out to those outside will lead to compromise within. So they choose not to build bridges. But Jesus built a bridge, reaching down to us and reconciling us to God.

We too must build bridges. But we cannot build bridges to reach those outside while we are building walls against our brethren who do not share our vision.

The problem is that it's easier to build walls. Bridges take much more work. Nevertheless, can we build stable bridges that will endure many years?

Stability, Ecumenism, and Exclusivism

We live in an imperfect world. We are constantly bombarded by influences that we wish we could avoid. We must acknowledge this painful truth: As long as we are here in the flesh, we will have to wrestle against negative influences that tend to destroy us. Christ fervently prayed, "I pray not that thou shouldest take them out of the world, but that thou shouldest keep them from the evil" (John 17:15).

For this reason, I don't want to write anything that would give the impression that I have all the answers. It is better that the church is not one physical organization. We should respect differences in application rather than opposing our spiritual brothers who do not view things the same way we do.

On the other hand, if I say that differences between church organizations should be appreciated and respected, I might be opening the door for differences of application to cross congregational boundaries. This would weaken the like-mindedness we need for stability.

We tend toward extremes. Time and again, a portion of the church has fallen into extremes because of overreacting to the extremes of another group. The old maxim "There's a ditch on both sides of the road" is still true. We may feel smug that we are not in a certain ditch, not realizing that we are in the opposite ditch. We need to strive for a balance that seems fragile.

Two extremes that can ruin a church are ecumenism and exclusivism. Each extreme can result from overreacting to the extreme on the other side. As noted in Chapter 11, ecumenism was one reason why the "Old" Mennonite Church apostatized in the middle of the twentieth century. And, as described earlier in this chapter, exclusivism affected the Dutch Anabaptists and the Jacob Ammann group so that reconciliation was not possible.

Varying degrees of exclusivism exist. One prevalent weakness is that exclusive churches tend to view other churches critically and cannot learn from them.

Churches that gravitate toward ecumenism may form ties with groups that do not share the same traditional values. This has a negative impact on the more traditional group and tends to destabilize a church. Some members begin to wonder what the point is in abiding by the policies of their home congregation, when members in other groups they associate with face no such restrictions. Individuals then lose an appreciation for their background. Even more alarming is when plain churches associate with Protestant churches that participate in war and government, tolerate divorce and remarriage, and do not see the need for living a separated lifestyle.

Therefore, leaders in a congregation need foresight to determine where to draw the line in associating with congregations that differ in practice from their own. To maintain our cherished values, we need to limit our association with groups where such values would be undermined and congregational stability threatened. We should still appreciate and respect other groups. We can always learn from each other. However, because of our understanding of the purity of the church and of separation from the world, we need to be cautious in relating to groups that would undermine conservative values. (The more liberal groups should also be willing to learn from the strong points of their conservative cousins.)

In conclusion, I share two concerns. We do not want the more-liberal churches to negatively impact us. On the other hand, we do not want to be exclusive. As a voice promoting evangelistic outreach, I do not want to oppose my brothers who see the matter differently. In all situations, we must build bridges, not walls.

Bibliography

Anonymous. "The Waldensians." http://www.thereformation.info/waldensians.htm, accessed 11/28/2016.

Anonymous. *The Walls That Divide Us*. Aylmer, Ont.: Pathway Publishers, 2008.

Bauman, Lester. *Exploring the Book of Acts*. Published 2003

————. *The Little Flock*. Crockett Ky.: Rod and Staff Publishers, 1999.

————. *Wolves in the Flock*. Crockett Ky.: Rod and Staff Publishers, 2001.

Beachy, Leroy. *Unser Leit*. Millersburg, Ohio: Goodly Heritage Books, 2011.

Bender, Harold S. *The Anabaptist Vision*. Scottdale, Pa.: Herald Press, 1944.

Bender, Harold S. and C. Henry Smith. *Mennonites and Their Heritage*. 1964. Scottdale, Pa.: Herald Press, Reprint 2000.

Bercot, David, ed. *A Dictionary of Early Christian Beliefs*. 1998. Reprint, Peabody, Mass.: Hendrickson Publishers Marketing, LLC, 2012.

————. *The Kingdom That Turned the World Upside Down*. Amberson, Pa.: Scroll Publishing Company, 2003.

————. *Let Me Die in Ireland*. Amberson, Pa.: Scroll Publishing Company, 1999.

————. *Will the Real Heretics Please Stand Up.* 3rd ed. Amberson, Pa.: Scroll Publishing Company, 1989.

Blank, Benuel. *Resurrection to Reformation and Beyond.* Parkesburg Pa.: The Blank Family, 2010.

Braght, Thieleman J. van. *Martyrs Mirror.* Translated by Joseph F. Sohm. Scottdale, Pa.: Herald Press, 1938.

Broadbent, E. H. *The Pilgrim Church.* 1931. Reprint, Port Colborne, Ont.: Gospel Folio Press, 2013.

Burkholder, David G. *Distinctive Beliefs of the Anabaptists.* Ephrata Pa.: Eastern Mennonite Publications, 2009.

Dyck, Cornelius. *An Introduction to Mennonite History.* 3rd ed. Scottdale Pa.: Herald Press, 1993.

Estep, William R. *The Anabaptist Story.* 3rd ed. Grand Rapids Mich.: William B. Eerdmans Publishing Company, 1996.

Eusebius. *The History of the Church.* 1965. London, England: Penguin Books, revised 1989.

Friedmann, Robert. *Mennonite Piety Through the Centuries.* Eugene, Or.: Wipf and Stock Publishers, 1998. Originally published at Scottdale, Pa.: Herald Press, 1949.

Giesbrecht, Ben. *The Enduring Church.* 2009. Reprint, Moundridge, Kans.: Gospel Publishers, 2014.

Gross, Leonard, ed. *Golden Apples in Silver Bowls.* 1999. Reprint, Lancaster Pa.: Mennonite Historical Society, 2014.

Hofer, John. *History of the Hutterites.* 1982 rev. ed. Reprint, Altona, Man.: Friesens Corporation, 2004.

Bibliography

Horsch, John. *Mennonites in Europe.* Crockett, Ky.: Rod and Staff Publishers, 1995. Originally published at Scottdale, Pa.: Herald Press, 1942.

Horst, Isaac. *Close-Ups of the Great Awakening.* Mount Forest, Ont.: Self-published, 1985.

Juhnke, James C. *Vision, Doctrine, War.* Scottdale, Pa.: Herald Press, 1989.

Lehman, Daniel R. *The Russian Mennonites.* Ephrata Pa.: Eastern Mennonite Publications, 2002.

Littell, Franklin H. *The Anabaptist View of the Church.* Reprint, Ephrata, Pa.: Grace Press, 2011. Originally published by The American Society of Church History, 1952.

Mandryk, Jason. *Operation World.* 7th ed. Colorado Springs Col.: Biblica Publishing, 2010.

Martin, Clifford. *Maintaining Biblical Conservatism.* Hagerstown Md.: Brotherhood Publications, 2007.

Martin, Donald. *Distinctive Teachings of the Old Order People.* Wallenstein, Ont.: Vineyard Publications, 2007.

———. *Joy in Submission.* Wallenstein, Ont.: Vineyard Publications, 2013.

Martin, Michael. *Cup and Cross.* Crockett, Ky.: Rod and Staff Publishers, 2005.

———. *Pilgrims and Politics.* Mazeppa, Minn.: Arundel Press, 2012.

McGrath, William. *Christian Discipline.* Minerva, Ohio: Amish Mennonite Publications, 1989.

————. *Conservative Anabaptist Theology.* Minerva, Ohio: Amish Mennonite Publications, 1994.

————. *The Mystery of Jacob Ammann.* Minerva, Ohio: Amish Mennonite Publications, 1989.

Menno Simons, Complete Works. Aylmer, Ont.: Pathway Publishers, 1983. Originally published by John Funk, 1871.

Müller, Ernst. *History of the Bernese Anabaptists.* Aylmer, Ont.: Pathway Publishers, 2010.

Packer, J. I., and M. C. Tenney, ed. *Illustrated Manners and Customs of the Bible.* Nashville, Tenn.: Thomas Nelson Publishers, 1980.

Philips, Dirk. *Enchiridion, or Hand Book of the Christian Doctrine.* Reprint, Aylmer, Ont.: Pathway Publishers, 2005. Originally published by John Funk, 1910.

Plain Things. March–April 2015. Caneyville, Ky.

Roth, John D., trans. and ed. *Letters of the Amish Division: A Sourcebook.* 2nd ed. Goshen, Ind.: Mennonite Historical Society, 2002.

Schaff, Philip. *History of the Christian Church.* 8 vols. 1910. Reprint, Peabody Mass.: Hendrickson Publishers Marketing, LLC, 2011.

Schlabach, Theron. *Gospel Versus Gospel.* Scottdale, Pa.: Herald Press, 1980.

————. *Peace, Faith, Nation.* Scottdale, Pa.: Herald Press, 1988.

Schrock, Elmer. *The Amish in the Shenandoah Valley.* Union, W. Va.: Yoder's Select Books, 2008.

Stoll, Joseph. *The Church and Mission Work.* Aylmer, Ont.: Pathway Publishers, 2008.

Verduin, Leonard. *The Reformers and Their Stepchildren*. 1964. Reprint, Sarasota, Fla.: The Christian Hymnary Publishers, 2013.

Weaver, Clair R. *The Swiss Anabaptists*. 1990 rev. ed. Reprint, Ephrata, Pa.: Eastern Mennonite Publications, 1999.

Wenger, J. C. *The Mennonite Church in America*. Reprint, Ephrata, Pa.: Eastern Mennonite Publications, 2003. Originally published at Scottdale, Pa.: Herald Press, 1966.

Wylie, J. A. *The History of the Waldenses*. London, England: Cassell and Company, c. 1860.